THE DIVINE COINCIDENCE

A JOURNEY OF FAITH, HEALING, AND MIRACLES

TIAN CHIN

Ark House Press
arkhousepress.com

© 2025 Tian Chin

All rights reserved. Apart from any fair dealing for the purpose of study, research, criticism, or review, as permitted under the Copyright Act, no part may be reproduced by any process without written permission.

Scriptures marked NKJ® are taken from the New King James Version®. Copyright © 1982 by Thomas Nelson. Used by permission. All rights reserved.

Scriptures marked ESV® are taken from The ESV® Bible (The Holy Bible, English Standard Version®), © 2001 by Crossway, a publishing ministry of Good News Publishers. Used by permission. All rights reserved.

Scriptures marked NIV® are taken from the Holy Bible, New International Version®, NIV®. Copyright © 1973, 1978, 1984, 2011 by Biblica, Inc.™ Used by permission of Zondervan. All rights reserved worldwide. www.zondervan.com The "NIV" and "New International Version" are trademarks registered in the United States Patent and Trademark Office by Biblica, Inc.™

Scriptures marked AMP® ares taken from the Amplified® Bible, Copyright © 2015 by The Lockman Foundation. Used by permission. lockman.org

Scriptures marked NLT® are taken from the Holy Bible, New Living Translation, copyright © 1996, 2004, 2015 by Tyndale House Foundation. Used by permission of Tyndale House Publishers, Carol Stream, Illinois 60188. All rights reserved.

Cataloguing in Publication Data:
Title: The Divine Coincidence
ISBN: 978-1-7642308-3-4 (pbk)
Subjects: REL012170   RELIGION / Christian Living / Personal Memoirs; REL045000 RELIGION / Christian Ministry / Missions;
Design by initiateagency.com

Table of Contents

Preface vii

Acknowledgments xi

Introduction xiii

Part 1: The Day the Lights Went Out

Chapter 1: Something About Sydney 3

Chapter 2: First Love in Kajang 5

Chapter 3: The Diagnosis That Changed Everything 10

Chapter 4: The Twelve-Month Ultimatum 14

Chapter 5: A Flight Toward the Unknown 17

Chapter 6: One Last Look 19

Part 2: When Nothing Happened

Chapter 7: Touchdown in the Valley 25

Chapter 8: The Waiting Room of Hope 28

Chapter 9: Dad Chased by Grotesque Demons 32

Chapter 10: A New Marrow, A New Dawn 36

Chapter 11: Perilous Challenge — Graft-Versus-Host Disease (GVHD)..39

Chapter 12: Masked and Fragile, But Alive 42

Chapter 13: A Ring, A Promise, A Return..45

Chapter 14: Return, Reunion, and Relapse 48

PART 3: HOPE FINDS A WAY

Chapter 15: Return to Sydney — The Fight Continues........................53

Chapter 16: Between Healing and Hope 56

Chapter 17: Still, She Stayed 58

Chapter 18: The Valley After the Light..60

Chapter 19: Breath by Breath 63

Chapter 20: Settling Without Belonging 65

PART 4: PUTTING LIFE BACK TOGETHER

Chapter 21: Kim's Leap of Faith 69

Chapter 22: A Risk Against Reason 72

Chapter 23: Crossing Paths and Cultures 74

Chapter 24: Before We Knew His Name 77

Chapter 25: When Hope Fights Back..82

Chapter 26: The Six-Week Mercy 85

Chapter 27: Grace at Every Turn 89

Chapter 28: Seeds of Faith and a New Calling......................................93

Chapter 29: Trials of Delay and the Faith to Persevere 96

Chapter 30: Detours of Disappointment and a New Season of Growth.99

Chapter 31: Waiting for a Breakthrough 102

Chapter 32: The Proposal and a Promise 105

Chapter 33: God's Perfect Timing 108

Chapter 34: A Covenant of Love 111

Chapter 35: The Wilderness Between The Promises 116

Chapter 36: A Promise in the Wilderness 119

Chapter 37: The Wedding We Almost Didn't Have 123

Chapter 38: Held by a Whispered Promise 126

Chapter 39: The Promise That Breathed 132

Part 5: The Ending I Never Expected

Chapter 40: The Unfailing Love of the Father 139

Chapter 41: A Father's Final Prayer 143

Chapter 42: A New Season Begins 150

Chapter 43: A Second Heartbeat 153

Chapter 44: A House of Blessings 157

Chapter 45: Bridges of Belonging 161

Chapter 46: Ambassadors of Reconciliation 165

Chapter 47: When Heaven Brushed the Ceiling – A Father's Night
of Revelation 170

Chapter 48: The Day of Decision 175

Chapter 49: When A Teacher Found His Shepherd 185

Chapter 50: The Divine Timeline 189

Chapter 51: The Divine Coincidence 192

About the Author 197

Epilogue: Forty Years of Grace 199

PREFACE

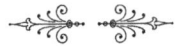

This book was never part of my life plan. In fact, much of what unfolds in these pages was never planned at all—at least, not by me. What began as a personal journal of thoughts, prayers, and memories slowly evolved into a tapestry of divine interventions, heartbreaking lows, and breathtaking moments of hope.

As I reflected on the decades that shaped me—from a hospital bed in Sydney to a life of ministry in Adelaide—I began to see that what I once dismissed as coincidence was, in truth, divine orchestration.

I wrote this memoir to remember—and to testify. To remember the faithfulness of God, who never once abandoned me, even when death knocked more than once. To testify of His grace, which turned a dying young man from Malaysia into a husband, a father, a grandfather and a shepherd of souls.

This is not only a story of physical healing through a bone marrow transplant—but of a spiritual transformation that no medicine could offer.

This journey is not mine alone.

It belongs to my beloved wife, Kim—my unwavering companion, whose sacrificial love, steadfast prayers, and unshakable faith carried us both through the darkest seasons. When others might have walked away, she stayed. She left everything familiar—her family, her country, her comfort—to walk a path that was uncertain, often painful, but always grounded in obedience to God. Her courage and quiet strength have been the anchor of our family and the heartbeat of this story.

It belongs also to my dearest sister, Lee, whose selfless act of love gave me the gift of life.

And this story belongs deeply to my beloved parents, who gave everything a parent could possibly give. They bore my pain as if it were their own, endured sleepless nights, made countless sacrifices, and never stopped hoping. Their steadfast presence—especially in the years when nothing seemed certain—was a living picture of unconditional love.

To countless friends, family members, and even strangers who became part of our story—each one a reminder that no one walks alone when God is at work.

God knows you. He formed you. He is growing something beautiful from your life. Even through suffering, He is producing fruit that will bless generations.

This truth is captured in the cover of this book, chosen with deep intention. At its base is a fingerprint—God's unique imprint on my life, a reminder that every detail of my journey was designed by Him. From that fingerprint grows a strong, rooted tree, symbolizing the faith, resilience, and restoration that came through years of trial and grace.

Hanging from its branches are three crimson pomegranates, representing the fruit of that journey—my three children, two of whom are joined by loving spouses, and one who is walking faithfully through a season of courtship. Each one is a cherished part of our family and a testament to God's grace. Together, they form the branches through which our grandchild already carries forward His blessing, with the promise of more to come.

The pomegranate, rich in biblical symbolism, speaks of abundance, fruitfulness, and covenant promise. This cover is not just artwork—it is my testimony in visual form.

PREFACE

Perhaps you're holding this book because you're searching for hope in your own season of suffering. Or maybe you're standing on the edge of faith, wondering if God sees you. My prayer is that these pages will not only encourage you, but invite you—to see the divine hand behind what the world calls coincidence. To believe that even your darkest moments can give birth to unexpected miracles.

This is not just my story. It is His story, written through mine.

Acknowledgments

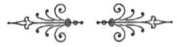

I am deeply grateful to the many people who have walked this journey with me. Your love, prayers, sacrifices, and encouragement have shaped not only this book—but my life.

To my wife, Kim—your unwavering faith, obedience, and sacrificial love are a living testimony of God's grace. You left everything to walk beside me, and your strength in every season continues to inspire me.

To my sister, Lee—thank you for giving me a second chance at life. Your selfless act was not only medically life-saving but spiritually transformative for our entire family. I will forever honour your gift.

To my parents—thank you for standing by me, even when you didn't fully understand the path I chose or the convictions I followed. Your quiet presence through the most painful years meant more than words can express.

To my children—Annabelle, Joshua, and Faith—you've taught me the depth of unconditional love. Born of prayer and promise, your lives are living proof that nothing is impossible with God.

To Peggy and Peter—your sacrificial kindness in opening your home when we had nowhere to go will never be forgotten. Your hospitality, support, and generosity in that vulnerable season sustained us.

To the doctors, nurses, and medical staff in both Malaysia and Australia—thank you for your skill, compassion, and perseverance. God worked through your hands.

To the pastors, mentors, and friends who poured into me, believed in me, and called out God's purpose in me—this testimony is yours as much as mine.

To our faith communities in Manly and Adelaide—thank you for covering us in prayer, walking beside us, and helping us find purpose in the pain.

And to the One who orchestrated it all—Jesus, my Saviour, Healer, and Redeemer—may every page of this book reflect Your glory.

Special thanks to OpenAI's ChatGPT and Microsoft Copilot for editorial guidance, structural support, and manuscript refinement. Your assistance helped me complete this book with clarity, confidence, excellence, and peace.

Introduction

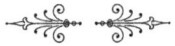

Life rarely unfolds the way we expect.

For me, what began as a promising future in Malaysia quickly took an unexpected turn—a life-threatening diagnosis, a desperate transplant, and years of pain, waiting, and searching. Yet through every setback, there was a thread of grace I couldn't ignore.

This book is a memoir—but more than that, it's a testimony.

A story of no faith, slowly becoming faith-full.

Of holding on when everything else was falling apart.

Of small miracles tucked inside ordinary days.

Of moments that felt like coincidence, but turned out to be something more.

The journey spans continents, cultures, and decades—from hospital corridors in Sydney to whispered prayers in Adelaide. It is a story not only of physical healing, but of spiritual awakening.

The chapters are arranged into five parts, each tracing a different part of the path:

- **Part 1: The Day the Lights Went Out** – when diagnosis shattered normal life and the future grew dim.
- **Part 2: When Nothing Happened** – years of silence, suffering, and learning how to wait.

- **Part 3: Hope Finds a Way** – small breakthroughs, divine appointments, and flickers of possibility.
- **Part 4: Putting Life Back Together** – rebuilding purpose, rediscovering joy, and serving from the scars.
- **Part 5: The Ending I Never Expected** – restoration, redemption, and a story only God could write.

This book is for anyone walking through uncertainty—whether you're facing a diagnosis, a detour, or a silence from heaven that feels unbearable. It's for caregivers, friends, and family who walk the long road beside the wounded. It's for believers whose faith is flickering, and for seekers unsure if God is real but willing to look.

You might read this in one sitting, or return chapter by chapter. Use it as a devotional, a mirror, or a lifeline in moments of doubt. Some may find healing in its raw honesty; others may discover faith in moments of divine interruption. However you journey through these pages, I hope you'll know this: you are not alone.

> This is not a story about escaping pain.
> It's about discovering purpose within it.
> Not about having all the answers—
> But learning to walk with the One who does.

> This is my story.
> But more than that—
> It's His.

PART 1

The Day the Lights Went Out

"The Lord is close to the brokenhearted and saves those who are crushed in spirit." —Psalm 34:18 (NIV)

Chapter 1

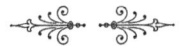

Something About Sydney

December 2005. Adelaide sweltered under a punishing sun, the temperature soaring past 37 degrees. That morning, our dear friends Andrew and Linda arrived with their children, parking outside our home for the long, two-day, 1,400-kilometre drive to Sydney.

I had always dreamed of visiting Sydney with my children. To me—and to my parents—the city held more than iconic landmarks. It held memories etched deep into our hearts: memories of pain, healing, and the miraculous.

Sydney was more than a destination. It was where God gave me back my life.

Out of gratitude and faith, I wanted my children to see where the miracle happened—to understand the legacy of hope woven into our family's story.

Andrew and Linda, who had lived in Sydney before moving to Adelaide, invited us to stay with Andrew's parents. It had become their yearly tradition, and this time, they welcomed us to join.

The drive, however, was far from pleasant. The blazing summer heat turned the car into an oven, even with the air conditioning on full blast.

The landscape was dry and colourless—a stark contrast to where we were headed. In one outback town, we stopped briefly. It was ghostly quiet, the streets deserted, as people hid from the 45-degree heat and the relentless swarm of flies that greeted us the moment we opened our car doors.

Yet despite it all, our children were bubbling with excitement. It was their first long-distance adventure. They couldn't wait to see the Opera House, the Harbour Bridge, take the night ferry rides, explore Darling Harbour, and visit the Blue Mountains.

But there was one place I was determined they must see: St Vincent's Hospital.

To them, it was just another building. To me, it was sacred ground.

It was the place that carried me from death to life.

It all began in August 1984—the year I finished high school. I had dreams: to become an accountant, marry the girl I loved, and start a family. My future was full of colour.

Then, shortly after I turned 21, that picture shattered. I was diagnosed with aplastic anaemia, a rare and life-threatening condition where the bone marrow fails to produce blood. Doctors gave me one year to live—unless I could find a bone marrow donor.

We searched desperately for a cure. Traditional Chinese medicine, Western doctors, Feng Shui, temple mediums, pastors—nothing worked. None of my eight siblings were a match. Bone marrow transplants weren't available in Malaysia. My time was running out.

But my parents refused to give up.

Clinging to the last fragments of hope, they brought us to a land we didn't know—believing, somehow, that in Australia, a miracle awaited.

And it did—at St Vincent's Hospital in Sydney.

Chapter 2

First Love in Kajang

Kajang, a small town roughly 20 kilometers from Kuala Lumpur, is home to the renowned Kajang Yu Hua Secondary School—widely considered the most prestigious school in the area. It's often the preferred choice for local ethnic Chinese parents, including mine.

Initially, my father had planned for me to continue at Confucian Secondary School in Kuala Lumpur after completing my primary education. But midway through my final year of primary school, he changed his mind. He transferred me to Yu Hua Primary School to complete my final months, ensuring a smooth transition to Yu Hua Secondary School after graduation.

By the time I reached Form 1 (equivalent to Grade 7), something unexpected happened—I developed feelings for a girl in my class named Kim. She was beautiful, intelligent, and incredibly capable. Not only did she excel academically, but she also held leadership roles in various extracurricular activities and served as our class monitor. She had presence.

As the years slipped by, my affection for her deepened, though I never dared to approach her. I was quietly infatuated, fantasizing that she might one day be my girlfriend—perhaps even my wife. But how could I ever win her heart? I was timid and unsure—just a quiet boy with wishful dreams. I'd steal glances at her each day in the classroom, only to blush when she caught me looking. She felt like someone from another world, while I was just... me. To make matters worse, plenty of other boys admired her too.

By 1982, our final year in secondary school had arrived. Paths were beginning to diverge: some students moved on to high school, others were sent to private colleges or overseas, and a few stepped directly into the workforce.

I was haunted by the idea that I might never see Kim again. On our final day of school, courage finally overtook fear—I penned her a heartfelt letter and enclosed a pink rose from my parents' garden as a graduation gift. Though the full contents of the letter have faded with time, I remember writing, *"I really like you."* I expected little more than awkwardness or discomfort in response, but felt I had nothing to lose.

To my astonishment, a few days later, Kim replied. Her note was brief but thoughtful. She thanked me for the rose and acknowledged my feelings with grace. One sentence lingered in my heart: *"The one who is loved is fortunate."* Her kindness eased my anxiety and planted a seed of hope—though it was accompanied by nervous uncertainty. How would I face her again? Would it be too awkward? I decided, for now, to let things be.

Three months passed, and our Form 5 examination results were released. To my surprise—and dare I say providence—we were both accepted into the same local high school for pre-university studies. Even more remarkably, we ended up in the same class.

For me, this felt like divine orchestration. For Kim, perhaps it felt like she couldn't escape me. Nevertheless, our daily encounters were tinged with embarrassment. I could barely make eye contact with her. Worse still, she often sat beside another male classmate who constantly chatted with her. I burned with jealousy and frustration, blaming my own lack of courage.

But I refused to give up. Despite the awkwardness, my resolve to win her heart only grew stronger.

I continued to express myself through letters, though they seemed to disappear without reply. Just as I was about to abandon hope, a longer letter from Kim arrived. It brought me immense joy. She wrote that she planned to nurture the rose I had given her so that it would grow beautifully and abundantly. Her words rekindled my optimism—it felt like a window had opened, urging me to act quickly.

I began telling classmates about my feelings for Kim. Part of me wanted to mark my territory: to let others know she was already "taken." Another part hoped to enlist their help in creating opportunities for us to be together. Some classmates did lend a hand, though it only deepened Kim's discomfort. Still, I pressed on. I may have been shy, but my determination was steadfast.

As a Chinese saying goes: *"One must be brave enough to venture into the tiger's den to claim its offspring."*

So, I took the risk.

Every morning, I would wait patiently by the back door of Kim's house, hoping for the chance to walk to school together. Usually, she rode her bicycle, but upon seeing me, she'd graciously push it alongside us, seemingly unfazed. Still, I suspected she found me somewhat bothersome—like a pesky Australian fly! At the time, social norms made it inappropriate for a girl to be seen walking with a boy on the street. And as a class monitor, Kim was expected to uphold exemplary behavior, especially while in uniform. But I ignored all that, content simply to be near her.

Eventually, Kim began leaving her bicycle at home and walked with me to school. Though the distance was only about a kilometer, I found myself wishing it were five—just to prolong our time together. To an outsider, it may have looked like we were dating. But truly, we were just walking to school.

Our routine soon evolved. I began walking Kim home in the afternoons, and before long, I found myself welcomed inside. I'm still not sure where I summoned the boldness to do so, but I ended up having lunch at her house nearly every day. Thankfully, Kim's parents were warm and hospitable.

One afternoon, my impatience got the better of me. A teacher had extended class time, and I worried Kim might leave before I could join her at the gate. As soon as the class ended, I bolted out of the room—and to my relief, there she stood, waiting quietly by the school entrance. I asked if she was expecting someone, and you can guess her answer.

When your heart's set on someone, jealousy isn't far behind. I became increasingly possessive. Anytime I saw other boys chatting with Kim or getting too close, I felt a surge of agitation. Once, a classmate cheekily covered her eyes from behind. I marched straight up to him and said firmly, "Don't you dare flirt with her again!" Of course, this protective outburst only made Kim more embarrassed.

Where your treasure is, there your heart is also.

I often gave Kim roses, many secretly gathered from our neighbour's garden. Buying flowers back then wasn't easy, and those unpicked roses would eventually wither anyway—so why not offer them to someone who brought colour into my life? I also started buying her breakfast, as she often skipped it before school—a habit that worried me. Only later did I learn she saved those meals to give to her younger brother. That act of selflessness made me admire her all the more.

Little by little, Kim began to show interest in me, even though other admirers still hovered. We grew closer—doing homework together, playing sports, even going out. Before long, it was official: we were boyfriend and girlfriend. My persistence had borne fruit.

We started dating. I took her to the cinema, followed by dinner at an upscale restaurant called Sakura. I hadn't realized how pricey their nasi lemak was—the most affordable dish on the menu still cost far more than the street vendors' version. I silently hoped Kim wouldn't choose the most expensive item. Mercifully, she didn't. My wallet survived.

Friday nights became my favourite. Kim had piano lessons at a nearby music school, and after her practice, we'd go for a drive and enjoy supper at a hawker stall. She paid for those lessons herself—saving her pocket money with quiet determination. I admired that deeply.

Once, I even let her drive my dad's new car, despite her being a learner. Looking back, it was a foolish risk—but I was willing to take it for her.

Some mornings, I cycled eight kilometres in the dark just to see Kim. We'd go jogging, have breakfast, and study together at her house. These moments were sacred to me.

One memorable trip to Port Dickson marked a milestone in our relationship. A friend taught me a cheeky trick to hold Kim's hand—beginning with her palm open, my finger tracing nonsense patterns as I told a silly story. Kim saw through the ploy, but it worked. We ended up strolling along the beach, hand in hand, for hours under the stars.

Our relationship blossomed. With Kim's support, I stayed focused on my studies. I dreamed of becoming an accountant, marrying her, and building a life filled with family and purpose—ambitions that any hopeful young man would carry in his heart.

But life had other plans.

And within months, everything would change.

Chapter 3

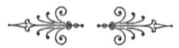

The Diagnosis That Changed Everything

My 21st birthday was celebrated at my parents' home—an uncommon honour in a family of nine children, where birthdays were typically marked with two simple hard-boiled eggs. In Chinese culture, eggs represent life and renewal, and while we never had cakes or candles, those eggs carried quiet weight—tokens of love, blessings for longevity, and the hope of another year.

But this birthday was different.

I invited many friends, prepared everything with Kim's help, and for the first time, proudly introduced her as my girlfriend. That day felt radiant—a celebration not only of age, but of love blooming under the gaze of family and friends.

Shortly after, while helping at my mother's chicken stall, a traditional Chinese medicine practitioner next to us glanced at me and said, "You should see a doctor." I dismissed it, blaming fatigue on a few restless nights.

But then the tiredness deepened—sudden, persistent, consuming. Badminton, once my joy, became an effort. My stamina disappeared. Red spots and bruises appeared like silent messengers across my skin.

My parents grew concerned and took me to a general practitioner. He diagnosed anaemia and prescribed iron pills. Weeks passed. I only worsened.

More red spots. More bruises. Nosebleeds. A cold that never left. My body dimming like a lantern low on oil.

A specialist's blood test revealed dangerously low red cells, white cells, and platelets. He ordered a bone marrow aspiration. The needle was thick and merciless. Even with local anaesthetic, it felt like steel boring into the heart of me. The pressure was suffocating—like my soul being vacuumed through a narrow tunnel. I clenched my teeth and gripped the hospital bed, refusing to cry out.

Then came a blood transfusion—a sudden burst of life. I felt restored. I even played badminton again. But it was fleeting. Within days, my colour faded. Weakness returned.

The diagnosis arrived: Aplastic anaemia. An unfamiliar name. An incurable illness. My bone marrow—the cradle of life—had gone dry.

The doctor explained: a drug, Oxymetholone might help to stimulate blood production, but hope was thin. Transfusions would offer temporary strength, but in time, my body would reject them. A bone marrow transplant was the only true lifeline—but a costly, dangerous one. Malaysia couldn't provide it. Options lay in America, Britain, Australia—but they were financially out of reach.

So we searched. Tried everything. Medication. Herbs. Temples. Altars. Feng Shui. Some said I needed a godmother to shield me from harm. They charted zodiac signs, measured doorways, prescribed rituals—and we followed every one.

A Malay shaman visited our home. His voice pulsed in low, rhythmic chants. Then he dug in front of our house. To our astonishment, he unearthed a yellow talisman with a rusted nail buried deliberately in the soil. "You've been attacked," he declared. "Not just physically—but spiritually." He handed me an amulet for protection.

My parents—frantic with worry—left no stone unturned. Every temple visited. Every ritual tried.

Eventually, a distant relative became my godmother. Ceremonies were held. But still, I declined.

Then came the Christians. They prayed. They spoke of a God who heals. I asked plainly, "If your God is so powerful, why doesn't He heal me now—to spare my family this suffering?" They prayed again. The illness remained. But they asked for nothing. The others often asked for payment.

Kim's parents collected wild herbs by the roadside. They boiled bitter brews with quiet care. Every act, however small, was a love offering. Still, I weakened.

Repeated hospital admissions followed. Doctors warned: "Avoid injury. Your platelets are too low. A simple cut could kill you."

Yet I refused to stop living. I sat for my Form 6 exams and earned grades that, under the circumstances, filled me with pride:

- Accounting: A
- Economics: C
- Mathematics: Pass
- Malay Essay: Fail

After school, my condition deteriorated. Blood transfusions accelerated—from monthly to fortnightly, then weekly. I spent 17 days in hospital. Kim came every single day—travelling over 30 kilometres to sit beside me from morning to evening. Even in illness, I felt like the luckiest man alive.

One afternoon, craving something beyond bland hospital food, I whispered to Kim, "Let's sneak out—I want KFC." We slipped into a taxi, laughing like rebellious teenagers. Halfway there, a nosebleed struck. Panic followed. We turned back, somehow sneaking in unnoticed.

No chicken. Just a reminder: even joy had its limits.

In three months, I received: 16 units of red blood cells and 4 units of platelets.

Chapter 4

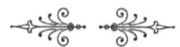

The Twelve-Month Ultimatum

Time was no longer measured in days, but in blood transfusions. Each one bought me a little more time, a little more strength—but only for a while. With every bag, I was reminded that without a bone marrow transplant, I was only delaying the inevitable. Death wasn't retreating—it was simply waiting.

Then came another blow: Hepatitis B.

It arrived like an uninvited shadow, carried in a tainted transfusion. My skin turned yellow. My eyes, hollow. My appetite vanished. I was too weak to protest and too tired to pretend I wasn't afraid.

The doctors said, "There is no cure. You must rely on your own immune system."

But I barely had one left.

I lay in the hospital bed—thin, frail—watching IV drips like hourglasses, counting not sand, but drop. Each one marked my decline.

My parents tried to hide their worry. Kim still came—every day—smiling through her fear, offering courage I couldn't muster.

We tried to hope. But hope began to feel fragile. It cracked quietly beneath the weight of bad news.

After weeks of Oxymetholone treatment without any sign of improvement, one morning, my doctor came. He spoke calmly, clearly, firmly:

"It is time to consider a bone marrow transplant."

The words hung in the air like thunderclouds. My breath caught. My mother's hands trembled beside me.

He explained, "The medication has not worked. Blood transfusions cannot sustain you forever. Your bone marrow has stopped. If you want to live, a transplant is your only chance."

We nodded. We already knew. But hearing it—plain and final—made it real. It stripped away every last illusion.

Then came the warning: Without a transplant, I had a maximum of twelve months to live.

The room fell silent. My father's eyes searched the floor for answers it couldn't offer. A sister turned away, stifling tears. I collapsed inwardly—grieving a future I hadn't yet lived.

We had believed the curse was broken after the shaman's ritual. That Jesus would heal. That Feng Shui masters held the answer. That temple mediums would offer hope. That a godmother would break the chains.

Each belief had offered its own kind of promise—action, tradition, mystery, miracles. But none brought lasting peace. We had placed our trust in everything and everyone, and still, death loomed.

My parents begged the doctors to contact St. Vincent's Hospital—a renowned centre in Sydney, Australia.

We chose Australia. It was closer than the U.S. or U.K., more affordable, and we had heard of Malaysian patients receiving successful transplants there. My aunt Lilian—one of my mother's sisters—lived in Brisbane with her husband, Uncle George. Though over a thousand kilometres from Sydney, they could help if needed.

The doctor wasted no time. He ordered HLA tissue typing for all my siblings to find a donor match. Among siblings, he explained, there's a 25% chance of compatibility.

We had nine children in our family—three from one mother and six from another, all sharing the same father. Surely one would be a match.

We waited. Each day hung heavy with silent hope.

Finally, the results arrived.

We entered the doctor's office eagerly, joyfully—certain we were about to learn who would save my life.

But the doctor's face told another story. He looked at us solemnly and delivered the devastating news:

> None of your siblings are suitable donors.

We were stunned.

Wasn't there supposed to be a 25% chance?

We sat there in silence—crushed. My future now hung on borrowed blood and improbable grace.

Hope, once fragile, now felt utterly broken. The terrifying shadow of death stepped closer.

Chapter 5

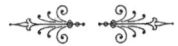

A Flight Toward the Unknown

The doctor urged us not to give up hope. He believed the test report might be flawed—that an error could have occurred—and recommended retesting. But my father didn't even entertain the thought.

To him, time was sacred. Waiting days for a retest when death loomed was unthinkable. Instead, he chose action: take five of my siblings to Australia and undergo fresh testing there. Even if the costs ballooned, the resolve of a desperate father refused to gamble precious hours.

Time was everything.

The doctor contacted St. Vincent's Hospital in Sydney, describing the urgency of my condition. With a referral letter and the hospital's response in hand, we raced to the Australian embassy to apply for visas.

Because of the critical nature of my illness, the application was expedited. Our visas were approved in record time.

Suddenly, the household sprang into motion—flights booked, winter clothes borrowed, old suitcases packed. It was our first long journey overseas to a country whose language, culture, and climate were all unfamiliar.

But this wasn't a holiday.

We weren't travelling for leisure. We were chasing a miracle.

Originally, my father planned to go with me and a few siblings, while my mother remained at home to care for the house. But just two days before departure, one of his sisters pulled him aside. She reminded him of the weight Mum would carry, alone with her worry and heartache. He reconsidered immediately—applied for her visa, booked her flight.

She joined us at the last moment.

Now there were eight of us. But that raised a new challenge: where could a family of eight possibly stay in Sydney?

In Australia, such a large household was rare. Rental homes that size were nearly impossible to find, and most required a one-year commitment—far too long for our uncertain timeline. Even the hospital's transplant housing had only three rooms and could host just one room per family. That meant space for only three people.

My parents were already carrying the weight of impossible choices—medical uncertainty, emotional strain, financial hardship, fear of the unknown. The housing dilemma added yet another burden. And now, my father's asthma began to worsen.

Then—almost miraculously—help arrived.

One of Kim's older sisters, Doris, had recently moved to Adelaide. She had a friend named Peggy who had just purchased a modest two-bedroom apartment in Randwick, New South Wales—right across from the Prince of Wales Hospital, and not too far from St. Vincent's.

Doris reached out, hoping Peggy might know of somewhere we could stay.

To everyone's surprise, Peggy offered us her apartment.

She hadn't known we were eight people—Doris had assumed only my father, the donor, and I would come.

Chapter 6

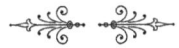

One Last Look

Two days before our flight, I had another nosebleed. It came intermittently, and with each drop, fear crept closer—I wondered if I would even be allowed to board the plane. Every time I wiped my nose, I felt like I was watching hope drain away. But just hours before we left for the airport, the bleeding stopped—and didn't return.

The airport was filled with a heavy kind of silence—the kind that doesn't come from the absence of sound, but from the presence of too many emotions. No one dared to voice the thoughts sitting heavy on their hearts. Relatives, friends, classmates, even a kind nurse who had once cared for me gathered to send us off. Their presence was comforting, yet each familiar face was also a mirror, reflecting the possibility that this could be a final goodbye.

They came to offer prayers, hugs, and words of strength. But beneath every gesture lay the same fragile truth: this journey wasn't guaranteed to end in return.

The operation I faced was high-risk. This wasn't a hopeful send-off—it might well be a final farewell.

Among them stood Kim.

She was quiet. Her heart was breaking, but she kept it tucked beneath the surface. Only recently had she come to terms with the depth of her feelings for me. And now, she had to stand at a distance, watching me walk toward a storm she couldn't enter. She couldn't follow me into the hospital corridors, couldn't hold my hand in sterile waiting rooms, couldn't care for me like she had before.

She was locked outside the storm I was walking into.

We had so much to say. But the words wouldn't come. Maybe there were no words big enough for what we felt.

Then came the final boarding call to Sydney. The silence cracked. Emotion spilled in quiet waves. One by one, loved ones reached for me—some clasped my hand and whispered strength. Others held me in wordless embraces, as if trying to memorize my presence before it slipped away.

I hugged my grandmother tightly. Her frail voice trembled as she offered words of courage through tears.

Then I turned to Kim.

I took her hand and gave her a single rose—a gift passed to me earlier by a thoughtful friend who knew I would need it. It wasn't just a romantic gesture. It was a token of hope. A message of love. A quiet promise that even in chaos, beauty had a place.

Through blurred vision and trembling lips, I looked into her eyes and said, "I love you."

I turned toward the gate.

But I hadn't taken more than a few steps before I heard my name.

Kim ran toward me, her sobs loud and unrestrained. She flung her arms around me and clung tightly. I held her just as fiercely, and we both wept—raw, undignified, real.

We didn't want to let go. The separation felt unbearable. Cruel. Wrong.

But I had to go.

I kissed her cheek, whispered once more, "I love you," and turned toward my waiting family. Their strength became my shield as we made our way to the plane.

I turned around one last time.

Kim stood behind the glass with our friends and classmates. Her face was buried in someone's shoulder, but her tears streamed freely. Many cried—not just for what we were facing, but for the love they had witnessed.

A love that refused to stay quiet in the face of uncertainty.

And as I walked down the long corridor toward the plane, strangely, I felt peace.

Death felt closer than ever—but I wasn't afraid.

And I never once believed I wouldn't come home.

When Nothing Happened

"Even though I walk through the valley of the shadow of death, I will fear no evil, for you are with me."
—Psalm 23:4 (NIV)

Chapter 7

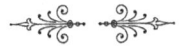

Touchdown in the Valley

In those days, flying was a rare privilege—something most only dreamed of. Boarding a Boeing 747 wasn't just exciting; it felt like crossing the threshold into a different realm. The flight attendants, graceful and warm, greeted us like honoured guests. For a family like ours, it was overwhelming—in the best way.

Once we settled in, cool towels were handed out. Safety demonstrations began. The engines hummed with growing anticipation—and then roared as we surged forward.

In under thirty seconds, we were airborne.

I had never flown before. Watching the earth slip away beneath us was surreal. Roads, rooftops, and trees shrank into patchwork. Somewhere under those clouds lay my homeland, my relatives... and the girl I loved.

We weren't flying for adventure.

We were flying in search of a miracle.

As we climbed to cruising altitude, calm surrounded us. Outside, it was minus sixty degrees Celsius. Inside, it was peaceful. My younger siblings wandered the aisles, full of wonder—finding joy even in airplane toilets and tiny bottles of toiletries.

The meals surprised us. Hot food, drinks on request, even complimentary alcohol. The flight attendants remained gracious and attentive.

But I couldn't enjoy it—not fully.

My thoughts drifted to Kim. I missed her terribly. Memories of her smile, her warmth, her presence played in my mind—but so did the moments I had hurt her. Regret settled heavy in my chest. Would I ever make it right?

Eventually, I slipped into a light sleep.

A soft tap woke me for breakfast. I lifted the window shade—and paused.

There it was: the first light of dawn breaking across the horizon. The sky glowed faintly, like a whisper from heaven.

A quiet sign that darkness had passed. A glimmer of hope. A new beginning.

Could my lucky star truly be waiting?

Soon, the captain announced our descent. Twelve degrees in Sydney. Back home, it was humid and warm. How would we face the coming cold?

On March 10, 1985, we landed in Sydney.

The aircraft halted, and an officer boarded to spray disinfectant throughout the cabin. We felt like potential threats—carriers of disease. The mood shifted.

At immigration, we fumbled with unfamiliar forms, trying to decipher the arrival cards. Customs was even more intense. Dozens of suitcases opened, searched, scrutinized. It made us feel like smugglers. Unsettling—but necessary. The officers were firm, but never unkind.

Outside, Peggy and her boyfriend Peter were waiting. Their eyes widened when they saw all eight of us. We did our best to explain—simple English, a few Hokkien phrases.

Still, they welcomed us with open hearts. They had even rented a car to pick us up. With so many people and so much luggage, some of us had to take a taxi.

Everything about Australia felt unfamiliar—the cool and fresh air, the quiet streets, the polite smiles. Drivers were patient. No one honked. People nodded in greeting. But understanding the accent was tough.

That first week was full of such funny misunderstandings—awkward at times, but unforgettable.

Our English was limited. Misunderstandings happened. Sometimes frustrating, often funny. Peter's Aussie accent was a challenge.

I'll never forget when Peter asked, *"How are you going to die?"*

I froze.

Turns out, he was asking, *"How are you going today?"*

Their apartment was modest—a two-bedroom on the third floor. What we didn't expect was that Peggy's younger brother, a university student, also lived there.

Space would be tight.

To our surprise, her brother offered to move out—taking residence in another property they had in North Sydney. What was once a short walk to university would now become a long commute with multiple transfers. It was an immense sacrifice.

Peggy asked for no rent—only that we help with the utilities.

We were stunned.

Two young people, building their own lives in a tiny apartment, offered us shelter with open arms and no conditions. My mother cooked for them daily. Peter loved every dish—his praise was endless.

We had stepped into the unknown.

But grace had gone ahead of us.

Chapter 8

The Waiting Room of Hope

The moment we settled into Peggy and Peter's home, they sprang into action. That same afternoon, they accompanied my father and me to the hospital to report our arrival. The staff reviewed my referral letter from Malaysia, and promptly admitted me for observation. Blood was drawn. Red cell and platelet transfusions were administered.

The effect was almost immediate.

Strength surged back so rapidly that I hardly felt like a patient anymore. Once I was settled into the hospital room, the sun had already shifted across the sky. I said goodbye to Peter, Peggy, and my father, then asked Dad to buy me some aerogrammes so I could write to Kim.

Though the hospital had been established in 1921, it was impressively clean, well-equipped, and efficiently run. But more than the facilities, it was the people who struck me most. The doctors and nurses were not just professional—they were kind. They saw me not as a case, but as a person. A friend.

I tasted fresh fruit juice and fresh cow milk for the first time. Even the Western meals—once a source of quiet apprehension—turned out to be so good I didn't miss rice.

After a comprehensive examination by the head physician, my siblings underwent HLA testing to determine donor compatibility. A few days later, I was discharged, instructed to return once an isolation room became available and a match was confirmed.

I had already written two letters to Kim.

Then came her reply—a letter penned just two days after I left Malaysia. In it, Kim described the heartbreak of watching me disappear through the departure gate. She wished she had boarded the plane with me.

Her words held more than comfort. They carried love. Strength. A quiet, unwavering purpose.

She urged me to be strong and to fight with everything I had. Her friends were keeping her company, and her mother—though concerned—was watching over her, making sure she ate and rested. It was a quiet, maternal expression of love, caring for the one who was caring for me.

Kim closed the letter with gentle wisdom: she encouraged me to be patient and kind with my family. She understood how easily illness could fray the spirit.

Her letter was a lifeline. It filled me with courage.

Soon after, Mom's sister, Aunty Lilian, arrived from Brisbane with her husband, Uncle George, and their newborn child. They brought laughter, new experiences—and a memorable introduction to stinky cheese.

One of their friends from Sydney treated us to a tour of the city. We explored the iconic Opera House, the Harbour Bridge, the bustling zoo, Chinatown, and the ferries crisscrossing the glittering harbour. Beneath the blue skies and crisp air, I felt something stir.

Could this place become home?

Then came the day.

The HLA results had arrived.

We returned to the hospital, our hearts suspended between hope and fear. The disappointment back in Malaysia still lingered in our memories. My life now hung in the balance—on a single report.

The doctor greeted us with a smile.

"Your sister Lee is a match," he said.

We sat in stunned silence. Tears sprang to our eyes. A match?

We had dared not hope too boldly—but here it was. Grace, pure and simple. One of our own. My sister. My miracle.

God had not only brought us across an ocean—He had gone before us.

The waiting room of fear had become the threshold of hope.

Relief flooded in like a wave. We were stunned. Joyful. Grateful.

The doctor explained I would soon be next in line for the transplant. Anticipation mixed with anxiety. I knew what lay ahead. Strict isolation. Chemotherapy that would wipe out my bone marrow and destroy my white blood cells. I would have no immunity. Even a simple cold could prove fatal.

As soon as we left the doctor's office, I ran to a public phone to call Kim. I shared the news and asked her to tell our grandmother. Our entire family clung tightly to this new thread of hope.

To celebrate, my parents took us to the hospital café. We decided to try Western food for the first time. My mother, uncertain but curious, ordered spaghetti—it was still noodles, after all. She watched a man at the next table sprinkle yellow powder on his plate and followed suit, thinking it was a seasoning.

It turned out to be Parmesan cheese—the infamous stinky kind. One whiff and she pushed her plate away. We burst into laughter. It became a memory we would cherish for years.

Before the transplant, I was required to undergo a sperm test. The doctor explained that chemotherapy could lead to infertility, and freezing healthy sperm was advised.

The results came back: I was already infertile.

At that moment, having children was the furthest thing from my mind.

I just wanted to live.

Soon, another patient was set to leave the isolation room. My turn was approaching.

But just before the procedure, another obstacle arose—my liver function had become impaired due to hepatitis. My bilirubin levels were dangerously high. Beginning chemotherapy now could cause permanent damage.

The transplant was delayed.

And so, I waited.

With time on my hands, I wandered through Sydney. I visited beach after beach, mesmerised by the clear waters, the softness of the sand, and the freedom carried by the ocean breeze. Australians loved the sea—and I began to understand why.

Curiosity even took me to Lady Bay Beach—a nude beach.

I didn't tell my parents.

It was a weekday, nearly deserted. Most people there were older. Ironically, I was the only one fully dressed.

No one said a word.

But I left quickly.

Chapter 9

Dad Chased by Grotesque Demons

My father had battled asthma for years. But ever since my illness worsened, stress weighed heavily on him. His attacks grew more frequent, more severe. Even with medication, relief was fleeting.

And because medical care in Australia was expensive, he refused treatment. Determined to save every cent for my operation.

Then, one afternoon—while I was still at home waiting for my bilirubin levels to return to normal—his condition spiralled.

The attack had begun the night before, but he hid it, hoping it would pass. By midday, he was clearly struggling. Still, he resisted going to the hospital. But as he entered the bathroom, he called out for my mother—and collapsed.

We rushed to him.

He lay unconscious on the bathroom floor. We carried him to the living room and gently laid him on the carpet. His eyes had rolled back. His fingers were stiff. He wasn't breathing.

Panic gripped the room. We were terrified.

Then somehow, through the chaos, my mind focused and remembered Australia's emergency number: 000.

At that time, I was the only one in the family who knew it—perhaps because of my own experience with emergency care.

I dialled immediately, explained the urgency, and gave our address. From the window, I saw the ambulance speeding toward us. Providentially, the emergency room was just across from our house. Within minutes, the paramedics arrived and burst into the living room with their equipment.

They began working on Dad right away. But nothing changed. His eyes rolled further back. His limbs stayed rigid.

We feared the worst.

They rushed him into the ambulance. I wasn't allowed to go with him. So I ran—across the street to the emergency department—where I waited alone.

My mother called Aunty Lilian in Brisbane, her voice trembling. Aunty Lilian wanted to board the next flight immediately. Soon, Mum and my younger sister Lee joined me in the waiting room. We were filled with regret, guilt, and fear. We wished we had taken him to the hospital earlier.

After what felt like hours—two, to be exact—the doctor emerged. His smile alone began to thaw the fear.

"Your father is stable now," he said gently. "He's breathing normally again. He's conscious."

Joy swept through us like a wave.

We followed the doctor to the emergency care unit. My father lay there, semi-conscious, connected to machines, a mask across his face. My mother wept—tears of gratitude and relief.

When he saw us, he looked confused. He didn't know where he was. He asked why he was in hospital.

Then he shared what he did remember:

> "I was being chased… by grotesque demons. They were everywhere. I ran and ran. I fell. Then, a bright light appeared. I heard a voice—clear and calm—repeating: 'It's alright, Mr Chin. It's alright, Mr Chin.'"

The doctors explained he had suffered a severe asthma attack, complicated by pneumonia—one that could have ended his life.

But somehow, he came back.

Once stabilized, he rested. We returned home and updated our aunt. She wept over the phone. She had feared the worst and had already booked the next flight to be with us.

Always mindful of cost, my father asked to be discharged early—worried about the medical bills and the money we had saved for my transplant. But the doctor insisted he stay. His pneumonia was still serious.

He remained in hospital for about a week.

And surprisingly—he loved it.

He enjoyed every meal. Western food! Compared to our crowded two-bedroom apartment, the hospital felt like a five-star hotel.

When he was discharged, we received the ambulance bill—over three hundred dollars. But the hospital charges? Zero.

A letter had arrived.

The pulmonary specialist who treated my father had written to the hospital board, explaining our circumstances: we were foreigners, here for my bone marrow transplant, saving every cent for that purpose. He requested all fees be waived.

They were.

Even more—the specialist never charged us a single cent for my father's follow-up visits at his private clinic.

Two months later, when Dad suffered another lung infection and developed pneumonia again, the same doctor arranged his readmission.

Again—no charge.

We were stunned.

Moved beyond words by the compassion shown to us—foreigners with no status, no wealth, no name.

Was it coincidence?

Or something more?

Perhaps grace wears many faces.

Sometimes, it speaks through strangers. Sometimes, it walks beside us in crisis. And sometimes—it chases away the demons we cannot face alone.

Chapter 10

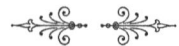

A New Marrow, A New Dawn

As my bilirubin levels slowly stabilized, the doctor gave the long-awaited green light: I was ready for the bone marrow transplant. The date was set—May 1, 1985. A day etched in my memory, wrapped in hope and shadowed by fear.

That morning, before heading to the hospital, I stopped at a public phone to call Kim. It was just past five a.m. in Malaysia. My call jolted her awake. But when she heard my voice, joy and anxiety mingled in her tone. She offered prayers, whispered encouragement, and sent a kiss across the ocean.

At the hospital, preparation began. Doctors inserted a catheter into a major vein in my chest—an access point for blood draws, transfusions, IVs, and the infusion of my sister's life-saving marrow. Though the procedure seemed straightforward, it required full-body anaesthesia. Afterward, I was moved to an isolation room to begin five rounds of chemotherapy.

The side effects of the chemo were immediate and merciless. Nausea. Vomiting. Diarrhoea. Appetite vanished. Even the smell of food from the corridor made me gag. Nutrients had to be delivered directly through the catheter to keep me going.

After my fifth chemo session, it was Lee's turn.

In the operating theatre, doctors drew roughly 900 millilitres of bone marrow from her pelvis. Oddly, she seemed to suffer more than I did. Pale and aching, she stayed a day in hospital before returning home—brave and selfless, without complaint.

Then came May 7.

A nurse wheeled in two large bags filled with crimson fluid. My sister's marrow. I stared at them, overcome with awe and gratitude. Her body would regenerate what she had given. But for me—it was everything. Without her gift, I wouldn't be here. I wouldn't have known Jesus. I wouldn't have witnessed His grace. I wouldn't be sharing this story with you.

Bone marrow transplantation, in practice, is remarkably simple. No dramatic surgery. No invasive incisions. The marrow was infused into my bloodstream through a vein, like a blood transfusion. And then—a quiet miracle. The new marrow instinctively sought out my bones and began to multiply.

Each day, my doctor checked my blood count, watching for signs of success. Eventually, white blood cells began to rise—a promising sign. After chemotherapy, my body should have been empty of marrow. So the emergence of new cells felt like resurrection.

Red cells returned. White cells multiplied. Platelets stabilized. My appetite crept back.

One thing, however, was missing—my hair.

I went completely bald.

Oddly, I found it quite cool. Still, I wondered what Kim would think!

With my strength returning, the hospital allowed visitors. Only those in perfect health. Gowns, gloves, and sterile shoes were mandatory. But each visitor brought more than conversation—they carried love, encouragement, and the kind of hope you don't find in a syringe.

I was healing.

And I was no longer alone.

Chapter 11

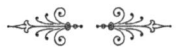

Perilous Challenge — Graft-Versus-Host Disease (GVHD)

The transplant had gone smoothly. My sister's marrow—her gift of life—had begun its quiet miracle. It was creating new blood cells within me. The first hurdle was crossed, and the doctors were encouraged.

But what came next was far more perilous.

Graft-Versus-Host Disease—GVHD.

GVHD is a medical paradox. It occurs because of immunogenetic differences between donor and recipient. The very immune cells meant to save you—particularly the donor's T lymphocytes—can mistake your body as foreign.

And then... they attack.

GVHD doesn't discriminate. It can strike the skin, oesophagus, gastrointestinal tract, liver, lungs—almost any organ. Relentless. Ruthless. For many, it becomes the most dangerous chapter of the transplant journey.

In most transplants, the host rejects the donor's organ.

But in bone marrow transplants, the opposite can happen.

The donor's immune system—now living inside the recipient—may reject the host.

In my case, it was my sister's white blood cells, now multiplying inside me, that could turn against my body.

GVHD is classified in two stages:

- Acute: within the first three months.
- Chronic: any time after that.

Acute GVHD can be fatal. Monitoring becomes a vigilant ritual—every symptom, every change, is logged and scrutinized.

To reduce the risk, I was placed on immunosuppressants. But it was a razor's edge. Too little, and the immune cells would rebel. Too much, and my organs might fail—while infection waited in the shadows to strike.

My blood counts looked promising. Hope lingered.

Then came the signs—subtle at first.

A rash. Itching. A deep, burning discomfort.

Then my mouth erupted with ulcers. My tongue scorched with every word, every swallow. Meals became agony. Even silence hurt.

Thankfully, my internal organs remained untouched. But GVHD had made itself known—and it wasn't leaving quietly.

The doctors moved fast.

They prescribed cyclosporine A—a powerful immunosuppressant. Added Prednisone—a steroid to ease inflammation and weaken the immunity. Prescribed co-trimoxazole—a strong antibiotic to ward off infection. And gave me an antifungal mouth rinse—to soothe what pain could be soothed.

It became a battle of chemistry inside me.

Every pill, every treatment, a soldier in the fight. The goal: help the donor marrow thrive... silence rejection... keep me alive.

The road ahead narrowed.

But I was still walking it.

And I wasn't walking it alone.

Chapter 12

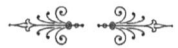

Masked and Fragile, But Alive

After 21 long days in isolation, my white blood cell count finally stabilised. The doctor gave the long-awaited nod: I could go home.

But this wasn't just a discharge. It was resurrection. A return not just to a place—but to my loved ones.

Our apartment was packed—ten of us squeezed into tight corners. Peggy and Peter included. Yet home had never been about square walls. It was about warmth. The quiet strength of family. The way laughter could fill a room, even when space couldn't.

If all went well, I could return to Malaysia within three months. But for now, I was still fragile—immunocompromised and vulnerable. I wore a mask. I avoided crowds. I became meticulous about hygiene. No raw food. No dairy. No shortcuts.

Still—one silver lining shone through.

I could eat Mum's cooking again.

Her lamb stew had always been my favourite. Especially sucking the marrow from the bones—a strange comfort for someone who'd just received new marrow. Thanks to the steroids I was on, my appetite surged. I devoured everything. And I began gaining weight fast.

But the medications had side effects. Water retention. Elevated blood sugar. Rising blood pressure.

And something else—the mirror didn't recognise me.

My face puffed up so dramatically, I joked I hadn't just had a bone marrow transplant—I'd had a face transplant too. Would Kim even recognise me? I laughed, but part of me winced.

The doctor reassured me. "It's temporary," he said. "Once the meds taper off, you'll return to normal."

One unexpected perk from cyclosporine: My hair grew back fast. Thick. Curly. Alive.

Still, the restrictions at home remained firm. No buses. No trains. No cinemas or markets. If I ventured out, I wore a mask. At home, every meal was a calculated risk. Every bite: reviewed, vetted, boiled.

Then, one day—I felt it. A slight fever. A tickle of a cough.

The doctor didn't hesitate. I was readmitted immediately.

Tests revealed a pseudomonas infection. Harmless to most. But to me—a loaded gun. IV antibiotics flooded my system. Thankfully, it worked. But it was a sobering reminder: I was still walking a tightrope.

My weekly rhythm now included outpatient visits. Chest X-rays. Blood tests. Endless monitoring.

GVHD had spared my internal organs. But it left its mark elsewhere—on my face. Dry mouth. Cracked lips. Painful ulcers. Even eating porridge felt like punishment.

At the transplant unit, I met others. Faces full of uncertainty. Some healing. Some not. But a few—shining.

One woman, Rosemary, had beaten leukaemia. She stood radiant. Joyful. Hope made flesh. If she could survive past five years, she'd be considered cured.

That became my quiet goal.

Still, old habits die hard.

One day, I gave in—bit into a small chilli pepper.

Instantly, my mouth lit up in agony. My heart raced. My face flushed. I bolted to the bathroom, rinsing with cold water for twenty minutes. Even then, the fire lingered.

It was a painful, unforgettable lesson: Not everything I loved was safe for me yet.

But I was alive. I was home.

And with every breath, every bowl of stew, every quiet evening wrapped in family—I was healing.

Chapter 13

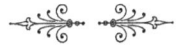

A Ring, A Promise, A Return

Living in a small apartment with all ten of us—including Peggy and Peter—was surprisingly harmonious. Peter, in particular, looked forward to my mother's cooking and eagerly came home each evening for dinner. Despite the cramped conditions, they never once complained. There were no deadlines. No expectations. Just grace. They offered their home without pressure—asking only that we help cover utility bills.

During our stay, we reconnected with a friend from our village—Ming—who had entered Australia years earlier as an undocumented migrant. She worked illegally as a cleaner and lived with her boyfriend, Fatt. Her mother and sister had followed, both seeking work without documentation. One found employment as a nanny, the other in a restaurant.

Though their movements were restricted, they found more freedom and joy in Australia than they had ever known back home. They lived simply, worked hard, and visited us often—with genuine kindness and warmth.

Kim and I stayed connected the only way we could: letters. There was no email, and international phone calls were costly. Each letter took about a week to arrive. Still, every envelope bearing her handwriting was a gift. I wrote often. Her replies came less frequently, but each one was treasured. Occasionally, I gave in and made short, expensive calls—just to hear her voice.

In one of her letters, Kim shared that our school friends had organised a fundraiser to help with my medical expenses. They raised over 3,000 ringgit—an incredible sum in 1985. I was deeply moved. That kind of friendship—thoughtful, sacrificial, enduring—is something you never forget.

One day, I spotted an advertisement for a beautiful ring in a magazine and decided I wanted to give it to Kim. I didn't know where to find it, but my parents and Lee searched all the way to Manly until they tracked it down. Their support for our relationship meant everything.

As my condition stabilised, my parents took a short break to visit my aunt in Brisbane—their first real rest since arriving in Australia, or perhaps since my illness began. Some of my siblings returned to Malaysia to resume their studies. My parents, worried about how swollen my face had become due to medication, asked them not to show Kim any recent photos. They feared it might distress her.

Only my parents and Lee—my saviour—remained to continue caring for me.

About three months after the transplant, with GVHD under control thanks to medication, my doctor gave the go-ahead: I could return home. There was hope that over time the GVHD would diminish. And maybe, one day, I'd return to Australia not as a patient—but as a visitor, with Kim and our future children.

Throughout my treatment, the hospital's generosity never waned. As foreigners, we expected towering costs. But they only charged us for my inpatient stay. Doctor consultations, X-rays, medications—even cyclosporine, which cost around AUD$300 per bottle and lasted only a few days—were largely covered.

The total bill came to about AUD$30,000. A significant sum, yet far less than we had feared. It was a blessing beyond measure.

As the date of departure approached, a quiet excitement stirred in me.

I was going home.

The doctor ensured I had enough cyclosporine to last, knowing it was unavailable in Malaysia. I still had medications to take. Precautions to follow.

But I was alive.

And I was going home.

Back to Kim. Back to where it all began.

Chapter 14

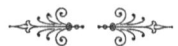

Return, Reunion, and Relapse

Finally, the day came.

After cleaning and packing, Peter and Peggy kindly drove us to the airport. Their kindness was beyond words—our angels in Australia. At the terminal, as soon as we stepped out of the car, I put on my mask and checked in. They stayed with us until we disappeared through the departure gates.

Gratitude overwhelmed me—for my sister, my parents, and every person who had walked beside me on this journey. As I entered the lounge, memories of the night I had left Malaysia flooded back. But this time, I felt anticipation, not fear. I thought of my grandmother, who had cried every time she cleaned our house, missing us with aching love. I thought of Kim, who was now preparing a homecoming meal—even learning a new dish just for me.

Back in Malaysia, my brother gently prepared Kim not to be too surprised when she saw me. She didn't understand what he meant—yet.

After eight and a half hours in the air, we landed. It was Malaysia's Independence Day. The timing felt divine—the beginning of something new.

At immigration, the officer scrutinised my passport, then my face. Again and again. I no longer resembled the photo. Thankfully, I had asked my doctor in Sydney to prepare a letter explaining the drastic changes.

Finally, we passed through. Lee and I stepped into the arrival hall. Everyone recognised me—except Kim. She scanned the crowd, uncertain.

When she realised the puffy, unfamiliar face beside Lee was mine, her eyes widened. Now she understood my brother's warning.

She smiled through the shock, took my hand, and whispered, "It's okay. You're back. That's all that matters."

We held hands quietly in the car. There was so much to say—but we didn't know where to begin. She needed time to process. And I understood.

Back home, our relatives had gathered. The mood was festive. My grandmother beamed, though she couldn't help remarking—lovingly—on how much weight I had gained. That night's dinner was a feast. Every dish tasted like celebration.

But the road to recovery was still ahead.

Returning home meant hoping for full healing—to live, study, taste spicy food again, and move freely. Yet GVHD remained, and time would be its healer.

At the local hospital, my doctor greeted me warmly. Reading the letter from Sydney, he quickly scheduled tests and follow-up appointments. I was his first post-BMT patient returning from overseas.

Soon, a sputum test revealed the return of pseudomonas—the same bacterium as before. My immune system, weakened by medication, couldn't fight it off. Though I had no fever, the doctor took no risks and admitted me for IV antibiotics.

Public hospital stays were free—my father was a government employee—but he feared infections in a crowded ward. So he paid out of pocket to transfer me to a private hospital, where the environment was quieter, safer.

Despite continuing the same medication from Sydney, my appetite began to fade. Food made me nauseous. I lost weight rapidly. My local doctor couldn't identify the cause.

Eventually, I contacted my Sydney doctor. He was puzzled too—but strongly urged me to return to Australia for further investigation.

Without hesitation, my parents secured a visa and booked a flight.

My journey—evidently—was not yet over.

PART 3

Hope Finds a Way

*"Those who hope in the Lord will renew their strength.
They will soar on wings like eagles."*
—Isaiah 40:31 (NIV)

Chapter 15

Return to Sydney — The Fight Continues

Everyone was surprised—and deeply concerned—that I had to return to Australia so soon. On February 16, 1986, I boarded a plane bound once more for the country that had already saved my life. This time, I travelled alone.

In Sydney, I stayed with Ming and Fatt—fellow countrymen I had met during my earlier treatment. They lived in a modest one-bedroom apartment, yet welcomed me without hesitation. Their home was cramped, but their hearts made room.

They took me straight to the hospital.

After a thorough examination, including tests for gastrointestinal GVHD, the results showed no damage in my stomach or intestines. But my liver told a different story.

Its function was poor—overwhelmed by the powerful medications I had been taking. I was fatigued, nauseous, and completely without appetite. The doctor adjusted my dosage immediately to prevent liver failure.

But just days later, Hepatitis B flared up again—this time more severely.

My skin and eyes turned a deep yellow. I had no energy. Even the thought of food made me ill. The doctor explained there was no direct treatment—only rest, hydration, and a strict, clean diet. With no effective Western remedy available, my friends urged me to consider traditional Chinese medicine.

I visited a herbalist in Chinatown—an elderly man with kind eyes and a gentle manner. He listened quietly, checked my pulse, and prescribed a three-day course of herbal remedies. He asked me to return for a follow-up and warned me to avoid alcohol, duck, beef, and greasy foods during the treatment.

That night, I brewed the herbs and drank the bitter liquid.

Within an hour, I experienced violent diarrhoea—unlike anything I had ever known. Alarmed, I returned to the clinic the next day. The doctor smiled gently and said, *"Your body is cleansing itself."*

Trusting his calm, I continued the treatment.

Physically, I was deteriorating. Ming and Fatt both worked and couldn't care for me round the clock. My doctor recommended that a family member join me. I called home.

My parents flew out as soon as they could.

This time, the hospital dormitory had a room available. We shared it with two other transplant patients and their families. It wasn't private, but it was safe—and we were grateful.

As my liver function worsened, the doctors reduced my immunosuppressants. But without the medication, my GVHD intensified.

It attacked my mouth and lips—dryness, ulcers, cracked skin. Every morning, I woke to find my lips sealed shut. Peeling them apart reopened wounds. Eating was agony.

Increasing the medication was not an option. My liver couldn't bear it.

The doctor tried PUVA—ultraviolet light therapy. It failed. My lips cracked deeper. Bled more.

Through it all, I kept drinking the bitter brews. Gradually, almost imperceptibly, my appetite returned. My mother cooked porridge and chicken soup. Even then, swallowing soft food brought tears to my eyes. The herbalist refined my prescription every few days. Slowly, the jaundice faded. My appetite strengthened.

Two weeks passed.

My father returned to Malaysia for work. My liver function stabilized. The doctors cautiously increased my medications—and this time, my body responded. The GVHD began to ease.

Two months later, I could chew soft food again. GVHD lingered, but it was manageable. The doctor was pleased.

He looked at me gently and said, *"It's time to go home."*

There was nothing more Sydney could offer.

GVHD, he explained, was unpredictable. No two cases were alike. It might linger for months. It might stay for years.

But I was no longer in crisis.

With careful management, I could begin the long process of healing.

And so, I prepared to return to Malaysia—not as a desperate patient, but as someone learning how to live again.

Chapter 16

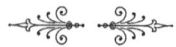

Between Healing and Hope

On May 10th, my mother and I returned to Malaysia, hopeful that this time, I could finally begin a new chapter in life.

But coming home wasn't as simple as stepping back into an old rhythm.

While my classmates were advancing in their studies or settling into careers, I felt stuck—caught in a limbo between recovery and the life I once imagined. Even something as simple as living normally felt out of reach.

And at times... I felt like a failure.

Lee, Kim, and my parents offered constant reassurance. *"Don't be impatient,"* they told me. *"Focus on getting better. Your time will come."* I nodded. I agreed with them in theory. But emotionally, I struggled with the quiet ache of being left behind.

Kim continued working at the bank in a modest role. It wasn't her dream job, but she stayed the course—determined to save for her future education. Her quiet perseverance stirred something in me. A spark. A question:

Could I return to college?

After two months at home with little change in my health, I saw an advertisement in the newspaper—an educational program tailored for high school graduates. I spoke with my parents. They gave their blessing.

I enrolled.

I chose to study Accounting, a subject I had always enjoyed. The school was new: HELP Institute (Higher Education Learning Philosophy). It offered a program affiliated with the Darling Downs Institute of Advanced Education (DDIAE) in Queensland, Australia. Students could complete their studies fully in Kuala Lumpur or finish the final year in Australia.

For the first time in a long while—I felt purpose.

But when classes began, a new challenge emerged: English.

I had studied mostly in Chinese and Malay. English had never been a priority in school. Now, it was everywhere—spoken fluently by classmates, woven through lectures, demanded in every assignment. I often sat in silence, too shy to speak. Too uncertain to contribute.

I became increasingly introverted—struggling to understand, reluctant to participate.

But despite the anxiety, I pressed on.

Healing wasn't just about my body getting better. It was about slowly rebuilding who I was—inside. Finding meaning again, little by little.

And maybe, by being back in a classroom, I could rediscover not only confidence, but the part of me I thought I'd lost.

Chapter 17

Still, She Stayed

September 1986 marked the third month since my return to school. One morning, while showering, I noticed strands of hair collecting around the drain. At first, I dismissed it. But day by day, the shedding worsened—my hair began falling out in clumps.

Soon after, my nails turned brittle and deformed.

A creeping dread set in: *Was the GVHD flaring up again?*

My doctor couldn't pinpoint the cause. GVHD was the most likely culprit, but he didn't want to alter my treatment while I remained on immunosuppressants. Samples of my hair and nails were sent to my doctor in Sydney. His reply came quickly and kindly—no signs of infection, no microbial cause. But still, no answers. He suggested I return to Australia for further testing.

Uncertainty weighed heavy.

My anxiety surged. My confidence collapsed. My studies suffered—and eventually, I withdrew from the course.

Within weeks, my condition worsened. Each morning, I woke to hair covering my pillow. Only a few tufts remained. One afternoon, I asked my mother to shave it all off. What little was left felt more like a fading reminder of what I was losing.

That evening, I put on a hat and went to see Kim.

The moment she saw me—bald, changed—the silence between us was thick. I needed her more than ever. But her reaction was quiet and withdrawn. Not unkind—just unprepared. I had arrived with no warning, no explanation. No space for her to process.

I couldn't blame her.

Still, her quiet discomfort echoed in me. I felt painfully alone.

On the drive home, doubt settled in. Was our love strong enough to weather this? Was Kim beginning to question our future too?

I pulled away. Stopped going out. Avoided people. Once, I had been confident and full of dreams. Now, I felt like a stranger in my own skin—a frail, bald, scarred version of who I used to be.

But Kim—despite the shock—didn't walk away.

Whether out of love, loyalty, or sheer determination... she stayed.

She visited often, bringing food, laughter, and warmth. I could see it weighed on her. Sometimes I pushed her away—refusing her invitations, declining to go out.

Still, she came back.

Her relatives began offering advice. *Why stay with someone so uncertain? Why not choose someone with a clearer future?* Even one of her brothers made subtle remarks about our future—expectations I couldn't yet meet.

I understood. I didn't resent them. If I were in their place, I might have thought the same.

And yet, every time I entered Kim's home, I was met with kindness.

No rejection. No harsh words. Just quiet understanding.

It was a time of doubt—but also a time of grace. Where love wasn't proven by grand gestures... but by quiet endurance.

Chapter 18

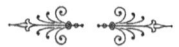

The Valley After the Light

I chose not to return to Australia for further examinations this time. The hair loss and nail deformed, though unsettling, weren't life-threatening—and the cost of another trip would've been substantial.

Still, I was trapped in a spiral of self-pity, shame, and guilt.

Yet Kim never pressured me. She only asked that I stay strong and keep focusing on recovery. Her quiet steadfastness became the reason I kept fighting—not just for myself, but for her.

To rebuild a sense of self-worth, Kim accompanied me to a wig shop in the city. The wig gave me a measure of confidence, though it never felt natural. I feared someone would notice… or worse, the wind might take it. Still, I wore it—not out of vanity, but for the fragile security it gave me.

A friend encouraged me to try tutoring high school students in accounting. He was already tutoring math and offered to help find students. Around the same time, Kim suggested we fry and sell cassava chips through a friend's mother's stall. I tried both. The chips didn't sell well—but tutoring gave me purpose and a modest income.

Six months after leaving college, I made a bold decision: to enrol in a one-and-a-half-year diploma in catering. My younger brother, Kong joined me. The course was offered by Kolej Damansara Utama and affiliated with a growing hotel industry.

Cooking was practical, creative, and hands-on. It carried less pressure than accounting—and felt more fulfilling.

We learned everything from knife skills to menu planning, nutrition to kitchen safety. For the first time in a while, I felt a glimmer of light—something to look forward to. Kim was thrilled. She imagined the day I'd prepare a Western dinner for her family.

It felt like I had finally climbed out of the darkness. Like I was walking in the warmth of hope.

Then—life turned again.

Two and a half months into the course, I noticed my eyelids drooping. I brushed it off. Then I couldn't smile properly. Chewing, swallowing—even speaking and breathing—became difficult.

Phlegm collected in my lungs. I couldn't cough it out. Climbing stairs left me breathless. I began sleeping upright. Drinking water sent it spilling from my nose.

My parents, heartbroken and helpless, watched their son slip once again toward the edge of life.

It felt like I had fallen into a valley deeper than the one before.

We prepared to return to Australia. The process—visa, flights—took a week. Too long, considering how dire my condition was.

Then, in a remarkable twist, my doctor called.

He had discovered a possible diagnosis in a medical journal: myasthenia gravis, triggered by GVHD. Clinical tests confirmed it. I was the seventh known case in the world.

Treatment began immediately.

Within two days, everything changed. I could smile. Swallow. Breathe. Speak.

Myasthenia gravis is an autoimmune disorder that causes muscle weakness—especially during activity. It affects the muscles controlling facial expressions, speech, chewing, breathing… even the eyelids. Rest improves it. Exertion worsens it.

Suddenly, my symptoms made sense.

Though my nails remained brittle and my hair refused to grow, I chose to stay. The medication worked, and I returned to culinary school.

It felt like I had found the light again.

But during the semester break, the symptoms returned. Breathlessness crept back—stealing even short walks. My medication dosage was increased, but it had no effect. The disease flared up again. Progress unravelled.

I had to abandon the course.

And with it, the dream I had fought so hard to reclaim.

I had no choice but to return to Australia.

It felt like life was testing me endlessly. Every time I climbed out of the shadows, I found myself in another valley—darker, deeper.

Yet still… I refused to surrender the light I had once seen. I believed it was still out there.

And I would keep chasing it— even if it meant walking through the valley again.

Chapter 19

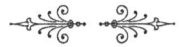

Breath by Breath

On September 5, 1987, my sister Lee accompanied me back to Australia for another attempt at rebuilding my life. The road ahead was undeniably difficult. Friends encouraged me to attend church upon arrival, suggesting that churchgoers were often compassionate and might help expand my social circle, improve my conversational English, and offer emotional or practical support. Though I had no intention of embracing the faith at the time, I figured it wouldn't hurt to go.

Thankfully, Ming and Fatt once again welcomed us into their modest two-bedroom apartment. Already home to six people, it now housed eight with Lee and me included. Despite the cramped quarters, their generosity never wavered.

Soon after arriving in Sydney, I met with my doctor, who referred me to both a neurologist and a pulmonologist. A battery of tests followed. The neurologist reaffirmed the diagnosis: myasthenia gravis, triggered by GVHD. This condition, along with GVHD itself, was also identified as the cause of my persistent hair loss and nail deformities.

More troubling, however, were the results of my lung X-rays. They revealed ominous white shadows, prompting further investigations — a CT scan, lung function tests, blood oxygen checks, exercise assessments, and eventually, a bronchoscopy. These raised the alarming possibility of pulmonary fibrosis. Though the bronchoscopy couldn't confirm the diagnosis or its cause, the specter of respiratory failure loomed. To reach a definitive conclusion, the doctors recommended an open lung biopsy.

It was an invasive procedure, involving an incision through the chest to retrieve lung tissue for examination. The prospect was daunting, but I needed answers. After two days of careful deliberation, I consented to the surgery.

The biopsy confirmed it: my lungs were damaged by GVHD. It was a crushing blow. I had hoped for a simpler diagnosis — something treatable, like a viral infection. But pulmonary fibrosis caused by GVHD meant irreversible scarring, and my lung capacity had already dropped to 50%.

The final conclusion was stark. The root of my hair loss, nail deformities, myasthenia gravis, and pulmonary fibrosis was a suppressed immune system — suppressed, but not enough. My body's new immune cells were attacking me. The only viable path forward was to increase the dosage of immunosuppressants.

I began a higher dose, and remarkably, within two weeks, signs of improvement emerged. My myasthenia gravis symptoms eased. A month later, my hair began to grow again, and my nails started to regain their shape.

There was no guarantee this remission would last. But for now, I was breathing a little easier — and I was still fighting.

Chapter 20

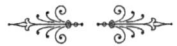

Settling Without Belonging

Lee started feeling bored, given that I didn't require special care at that time. To contribute to our living expenses, she ventured out to find a job even though her visa didn't permit work in Australia. To our surprise, she quickly landed a temporary position as a shop assistant at a fish shop. Working around ten hours a week, she earned just enough to cover our living expenses — and enjoyed discounted seafood in the process.

Soon after, through a friend's recommendation, Lee secured a more stable job at an envelope factory. It was far from home, requiring two bus rides and over an hour of commuting each way. Still, she was grateful and worked diligently. Her schedule was full-time, Monday through Friday, with occasional overtime that helped stretch her income. Her determination to support us, despite the obstacles, was deeply moving.

On weekends and holidays, Ming, Fatt, and their friends would invite us to join them for outings or movies. These moments lifted our spirits and eased the ache of homesickness. In truth, all of us were foreigners living in uncertainty, without residency status. That shared vulnerability fostered a quiet but powerful sense of solidarity, mutual care, and resilience.

Many held onto the hope that the Australian government might one day grant amnesty to undocumented migrants. But caution prevailed. The fear of being discovered and deported was ever-present. Everyone lived simply, saved diligently, and planned for both hope and hardship.

Around that time, I began attending worship services at a nearby church — not out of religious conviction, but more out of curiosity, and perhaps a quiet search for community. Friends back in Malaysia had suggested that churches in Australia might offer kindness, conversation, and connection.

To be honest, the experience was underwhelming at first. I struggled to understand the pastor's sermons and found the hymns uninspiring. My real hope had been to meet people, practice English, and feel less isolated. Fatt teased that I was going to church to meet girls — but most of the congregation was elderly.

As the only Asian in the church, with poor English and a shy disposition, I rarely lingered after services. I usually slipped out quietly before the final amen.

Still, I kept going. Not because I found God, but because part of me was hoping something — or someone — might find me.

PART 4

Putting Life Back Together

"He lifted me out of the slimy pit, out of the mud and mire; he set my feet on a rock and gave me a firm place to stand."
—Psalm 40:2 (NIV)

Chapter 21

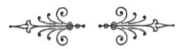

Kim's Leap of Faith

In the 1980s, the Australian government continued to offer scholarships to Malaysian students, and 1987 marked the final year of the program. When Kim came across this news in the newspaper, she felt a spark of possibility and decided to sit for the examination.

To her surprise and joy, she passed — and was awarded a rare half scholarship. The news brought a rush of mixed emotions. While she was thrilled at the opportunity for further education, she also worried deeply about how she would afford the remaining tuition and living expenses. Her family simply didn't have the financial means to support her.

Her father was hesitant. On one hand, he felt guilty that he couldn't help financially. On the other, he questioned whether it made sense for Kim — already 24 years old — to return to full-time study. In Malaysia, it was uncommon for someone her age to re-enter the education system. Worse still, her scholarship required her to complete a year of Year 12 studies before even beginning university, making it a four-year commitment.

To complicate things further, rumours swirled. People assumed she was choosing Australia not for academics, but to be near me. The judgment stung, and Kim found herself torn between ambition, practicality, and the expectations of others.

In the midst of this emotional storm, her sister Jo — a devoted Christian — invited her to church. It was Kim's first time attending a worship service. As soon as she stepped inside, something broke open inside her. Tears streamed down her face, unbidden and unstoppable. She didn't understand why she was crying, but afterward, she felt a lightness she hadn't known in months. A burden had lifted.

When she got home, still seeking clarity, she opened a Bible for the first time. She flipped it open randomly and landed on the Gospel of John, chapter 2 — the story of Jesus turning water into wine. As she read, it felt like the words leapt off the page and into her heart. She sensed God whispering to her: "Pour yourself in like water, and I will turn you into wine."

Soon after, her sister Doris in Adelaide called. Without knowing what Kim had read or felt, Doris offered to help pay her first year's school fees — and welcomed her to stay at her house. Everything began falling into place. Kim accepted the scholarship, and for the first time, she believed it wasn't simply fate or coincidence — but divine guidance.

In January 1988, Kim used her savings to buy a plane ticket and arrived in Adelaide with $1,000 AUD in hand and a heart full of hope. She began her new life as a student. Her sister helped her settle in and connected her to two restaurant jobs — one at a friend's place, another at a cousin's — that helped cover her expenses.

At 24, she was the oldest student in her Year 12 class. At first, classmates assumed she was only 17 — her youthful appearance deceiving everyone. When she revealed her actual age, they were stunned.

Australian student life was a culture shock. Kim was amazed at how casually students addressed their teachers by first names, used profanity openly, and even smoked during breaks. There was little of the rigid discipline she had known back home.

One of her cousins, also a Christian, introduced her to a lively and welcoming church. Kim quickly found joy in the vibrant worship and began to feel a deeper connection to the faith she had only just begun to explore.

Juggling classes and work was exhausting, but Kim persevered. Her resilience showed through in every task she took on. Within a year, she had not only completed her Year 12 studies but saved enough to begin her university program in accounting.

She had made her leap — not just across oceans, but into a future she once thought was out of reach. Her 'water' was turning into wine.

Chapter 22

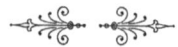

A Risk Against Reason

Over time, my health saw a remarkable turnaround. My myasthenia gravis was finally under control, and my strength steadily returned. I could climb to the third floor without feeling exhausted. My hair began to grow back, and the deformation in my nails had significantly improved. Follow-up appointments, once twice a week, were gradually reduced to weekly, and then to monthly visits.

With these improvements came an unavoidable question: what now? What was the next step for my future?

As my GVHD stabilized, I seriously considered returning to Malaysia. But the thought was fraught with fear. I knew Malaysia lacked the experience and research expertise to manage GVHD effectively. Going back could mean wasted effort, soaring expenses, and the risk of complications I might not survive.

I had already endured two terrifying relapses—both critical, both life-threatening. I couldn't afford a third. Harder still, I no longer had the confidence to resume my studies there. What once felt familiar now felt uncertain. The future in Malaysia, once full of promise, now looked dim and distant.

Staying in Australia, though uncertain, seemed like the only viable path — a chance to build something, to survive with purpose. Yet becoming a permanent resident felt like an impossible dream. One immovable barrier loomed: my health.

Even if I had desirable skills or qualifications, I wouldn't pass the mandatory health exam for residency. Still, I had to try. I visited the immigration office and explained my situation in full. The officer listened patiently and then gently laid out the harsh reality: my application wouldn't stand a chance. He advised me not to waste money applying.

Refusing to give up, I turned to the Sydney Chinese Community Association and the hospital's social workers. They showed kindness and tried to advocate on my behalf. But the answer from immigration was still the same: a polite but definitive "no."

There was, however, a thin silver lining. Immigration was willing to extend my temporary visa — but only for ongoing medical treatment. The condition: I wouldn't be allowed to work or study.

I was crushed. I felt helpless. I was a guest in a country that couldn't grant me a future, and yet I had no future waiting for me back home either.

And yet — somewhere within me — there was peace. A strange, quiet certainty that I couldn't explain. An inner voice said, "Apply anyway." It made no sense. But the feeling was clear: Don't give up. Something is about to change.

Was it faith? Delusion? Or something in between?

I chose to listen.

Chapter 23

Crossing Paths and Cultures

By now, Lee and I had spent six months in Australia. Our visas had been extended twice, reaching the maximum allowable extension of one year. While we initially got along well with Ming and Fatt, misunderstandings later emerged, prompting us to find a place of our own. Coincidentally, their lease was ending, and they were planning to relocate.

Around that time, one of Lee's colleagues introduced her to a friend who lived near her workplace. This new friend graciously invited Lee to stay temporarily in her one-bedroom apartment. However, as a man, it wasn't appropriate for me to stay there too. With time pressing, and uncertainty looming over our housing situation, we made a quick decision: Lee would move in with her friend while I travelled to Adelaide to see Kim and attend her sister's wedding.

Back then, domestic airfares were expensive. A round-trip from Sydney to Adelaide cost around five to six hundred dollars. Opting for the more economical route, I booked a seventeen-hour long-distance bus ride. It was a gruelling journey, but when love awaits at the other end, no distance feels too far.

The driver made several stops for food and rest breaks, and at one point, another driver took over. The bus ride allowed me to witness the raw beauty of Australia's countryside: rolling plains, rugged wilderness, and charming rural towns. Adelaide, in contrast to Sydney's hilly terrain, sprawled across a plain. With its modest skyline and slower pace, I affectionately dubbed it a "Village Town."

The city's charm lay in its simplicity. Friendly locals, short commutes, and an abundance of historic churches earned it the name "City of Churches." For locals, any journey over fifteen minutes was considered too far — a notion I found amusing.

When I finally arrived, Kim was there to greet me. Our reunion in Australia felt surreal. We were thrilled to see each other again. Kim had put on a little weight from her time in Australia, which she laughed about. My new hairstyle — or rather, lack of one — also caught her by surprise.

There was much to say, yet neither of us knew where to begin. We spent our days exploring Adelaide together. Kim drove me around in her sister's old Beetle, visiting her school, Chinatown, Hahndorf (a quaint German village), scenic hills, churches, and beaches. It brought back memories of Malaysia, where we had driven around in my father's Beetle during our school days.

Kim gave me a Bible and encouraged me to read it whenever I felt the need. Though not deeply religious at the time, her experience at church and her sense of divine guidance had left a lasting impression.

After her sister's wedding, I took the opportunity to visit Rosemary, a fellow bone marrow transplant survivor I had met at the hospital in Sydney. She happened to be in Adelaide visiting her mother, whom I had also met. Rosemary and I had kept in touch by mail since our recoveries.

She and her husband invited Kim and me to dinner at the casino's upscale restaurant. However, I didn't realize sneakers were inappropriate attire. I was turned away at the entrance. Embarrassed, I watched helplessly as Rosemary's husband drove 40 minutes round-trip to fetch a spare pair of leather shoes for me.

It was our first experience in such an elegant setting. The live music, polished decor, and romantic atmosphere left me awestruck. I wished we had the place to ourselves.

Dinner was a lavish buffet. I had never tasted such rich and varied delicacies: plump oysters, prawns, seafood, savoury meats, and salads that were surprisingly delicious. The dessert counter was irresistible. Though I had eaten earlier, I couldn't resist indulging. My appetite surprised everyone. Eventually, I had to stop myself for fear of vomiting!

When the bill arrived, I was prepared to thank Rosemary and her husband for treating us — only to discover that everyone was contributing their share. It was my first time encountering this custom. In my culture, an invitation implied the host would pay. Thankfully, I had exactly fifty dollars in my wallet. The experience taught me that in Australia, dining together didn't always mean someone else was footing the bill.

Though unfamiliar, I came to appreciate this custom. But for newcomers like Kim and me, it could certainly be an awkward surprise. Even birthday parties or family dinners might come with separate bills. It was a cultural adjustment, but one more step in understanding life in a foreign land.

Chapter 24

Before We Knew His Name

After spending approximately a month in Adelaide, I returned to Sydney and temporarily stayed at Lee's colleague's house. She too was an undocumented immigrant, but despite lacking legal residency, her children could still attend public school — a small mercy in a difficult life. I slept on their living room sofa, and the next day, I began my search for a place to live.

Renting a house was no easy feat. Landlords demanded references, proof of rental history, income statements, and more. To make matters worse, I had no familiarity with the area and didn't even know where to begin looking.

Early the next morning, I set out after breakfast, my heart heavy with worry and uncertainty. Where would I find a house? Would anyone be willing to rent to us? While waiting for the bus, I remembered the Bible Kim had given me. She had told me to read it when I was anxious or lost. Desperate and unsure, I took it from my backpack and opened it at random.

I landed on Matthew 6:25–34 (NIV):

> 25 "Therefore I tell you, do not worry about your life, what you will eat or drink; or about your body, what you will wear. Is not life more than food, and the body more than clothes?
>
> 26 Look at the birds of the air; they do not sow or reap or store away in barns, and yet your heavenly Father feeds them. Are you not much more valuable than they?
>
> 27 Can any one of you by worrying add a single hour to your life? 28 "And why do you worry about clothes? See how the flowers of the field grow. They do not labor or spin.
>
> 29 Yet I tell you that not even Solomon in all his splendor was dressed like one of these.
>
> 30 If that is how God clothes the grass of the field, which is here today and tomorrow is thrown into the fire, will he not much more clothe you—you of little faith?
>
> 31 So do not worry, saying, 'What shall we eat?' or 'What shall we drink?' or 'What shall we wear?'
>
> 32 For the pagans run after all these things, and your heavenly Father knows that you need them.
>
> 33 But seek first his kingdom and his righteousness, and all these things will be given to you as well.
>
> 34 Therefore do not worry about tomorrow, for tomorrow will worry about itself. Each day has enough trouble of its own."

The words struck me with startling relevance. They felt written just for me — as if the Bible knew the exact condition of my heart. I wasn't a Christian, hadn't prayed, hadn't read the Bible before, yet here I was, feeling comforted and strangely confident.

I had planned to take the bus to Manly to look for rental signs. But after reading that passage, I felt an unexplainable nudge to walk instead — a journey that would take 45 minutes. Trusting that intuition, I started walking.

Barely five minutes later, I stumbled upon a row of shops — one of which was a real estate agency. That coincidence felt almost scripted. I entered and asked if there were any available rentals. The agent, surprisingly friendly, told me there was a two-bedroom apartment nearby. He even offered to drive me there.

The apartment was ideal — clean, quiet, close to the bus stop and supermarket, and perfect for Lee's commute. The rent was a bit steep, half of Lee's weekly salary, but the location made it worthwhile. I returned to the office, filled out the forms, and to my astonishment, the agent agreed to rent it to me on the spot — no referees, no rental history. Just like that.

Was it just coincidence? Or was it what Kim had spoken of — divine intervention? Why did I even care to bring the Bible with me in my backpack that morning? And why did my very first time opening it lead me straight to Matthew 6:25–34 (NIV) — a passage that spoke so precisely to my anxious heart? *"Therefore I tell you, do not worry about your life…"* The words felt alive, as if they were written for that exact moment. I couldn't shake the sense that something greater was at work. Even Lee loved the apartment, and we moved in the very next day after setting up the utilities.

Three weeks later, our cousin and his family of three moved in with us. They had come from Wagga Wagga, 460 kilometres away, seeking better opportunities. Also undocumented, they found hope in Sydney and brought with them a willingness to share the rent and burdens. Their arrival eased our financial worries.

Looking back, I came to recognize something I couldn't see at the time: this was the love of God. Our Heavenly Father had been caring for us long before we ever knew how to call on His name.

His provision was quiet but precise — timely shelter, unexpected companionship, and unwavering support. At first, I might have called them lucky breaks or fortunate timing. But they weren't coincidences. They were grace. The kind that slips in unannounced, arranging details we never thought to pray for.

Later, I came to understand: God's love is not dependent on our awareness of Him. He doesn't wait for our faith to be perfect before He begins to act. Even before we knew Him, He knew us. He saw our fears. He anticipated our needs. And He stepped in — not only to provide, but to comfort, guide, and draw us near.

In those early days, I would sometimes feel a strange certainty about a decision or a sudden peace about a situation. I dismissed it as intuition, or what people call a "sixth sense." But now I know — it was the touch of the Holy Spirit.

If not for that inner nudge, I would've gone with my original plan: taken the bus to Manly, worn myself out chasing options, and likely missed the house that ended up being such a perfect fit. That guidance wasn't logic. It wasn't chance. It was God's gentle direction through His Spirit — leading, prompting, shielding.

And it didn't stop there.

In what felt like perfect timing, our cousin's family was also 'led' to move in and share the rent. Another coincidence? No. It was care. From a Father who not only sees the big picture, but also paints in fine, delicate strokes.

Whether you call it faith or fortune, I came to a place where I could no longer deny it: something greater — Someone greater — was watching over us. Guiding the details. Catching the tears. Providing, even when we didn't yet know who to thank.

He comforted us before we ever cried out to Him.

And when we did seek Him — He answered.

Chapter 25

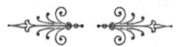

When Hope Fights Back

Once everything had settled, my next task was to prepare the documentation for my permanent residency application. I carefully composed a statement outlining the reasons behind my request. In addition to obtaining reports from doctors in both Malaysia and Australia detailing my medical challenges, I reached out to friends in Australia — including Rosemary and her mother — to provide personal testimonies and recommendation letters in support of my case.

With all the documents in hand, on June 9, 1988, I engaged an immigration agent to submit my application under compassionate and humanitarian grounds. Despite having already been verbally rejected by immigration officials, the agent — after a lengthy phone conversation with someone in Canberra — confidently assured me of the application's approval. He boldly asserted that it could happen. I wasn't sure if he truly believed that—or if he was simply saying it to secure my business.

After submitting the application, the days of waiting grew monotonous. Lee went to work while I stayed home alone, battling frustration and a growing sense of purposelessness. I longed to study or work — anything to enrich my life — but my visa strictly prohibited both. The fear of deportation if caught breaking the rules was very real.

To ease my confinement, I began taking walks along the coastal hills near our home. The breathtaking views of Sydney's outer harbor brought moments of peace and beauty. On weekends, Lee and I would stroll together in those same areas.

On Sundays, we sometimes attended a local church. Though the congregation was warm and often invited us to join in fellowship, we struggled to understand the sermons and couldn't connect due to our limited English. We weren't quite sure why we kept going — perhaps God was gently drawing us, even though we didn't fully realize it yet.

During that winter, boredom and restlessness led me down a dangerous path. One day at the supermarket, I discovered I could switch price tags from cheaper items onto more expensive ones. It felt thrilling to outsmart the system. The trick was easy and, at first, harmless in my eyes — until I escalated to hiding a chocolate bar in my coat pocket and walking out without paying. The adrenaline rush made me feel alive. Suddenly, my days had purpose — an exciting, secret purpose.

I rationalized my actions. Security was lax — it was their fault for not catching me. My coat's thick winter fabric concealed everything. I even made it a point to buy a cheap item or two to deflect suspicion. I convinced myself it was a game, a harmless challenge. Lee and Kim had no idea what I was doing.

But over time, the thrill faded, replaced by guilt. My conscience stirred — quietly at first, then louder with each theft. Eventually, the guilt became unbearable. I started returning stolen items to the shelves or discarding them altogether. I couldn't understand my own behaviour — willing to steal, yet too ashamed to enjoy what I took.

Reflecting now, I see God's hand in those moments. He protected me from being caught and deported. More importantly, He convicted me of my wrongdoing — not through punishment, but through the quiet, persistent voice of the Holy Spirit. It was that same Spirit who had guided me to the Bible when I was searching for a house. Now, He was guiding me again, calling me to repentance and integrity.

Eventually, I stopped stealing altogether. I understood that what I thought was merely a game was in fact a moral test. Had I ignored that inner voice, the consequences could have been disastrous. I am deeply grateful that God didn't abandon me in my foolishness — but instead used even my mistakes to teach me and draw me closer to Him.

Chapter 26

The Six-Week Mercy

About a month and a half after submitting my immigration application, the phone rang.

An immigration officer invited me for an interview. My heart raced — not with fear, but with that flicker of hope that clings to uncertainty. During our conversation, he asked about my health and who was providing for me financially. I saw a small opening and took it. I asked if I could apply for a study permit while waiting for the outcome of my application.

To my surprise, just a few days later, the immigration office granted it.

It felt like a window had cracked open.

But the breeze of hope was brief. It wasn't the beginning of a new academic year, so I couldn't enrol in any classes. Worse, I hesitated. What if I started something, only to have my application rejected? Still, the study permit itself was something — a whisper that maybe, just maybe, my case was being considered.

Two weeks later, I was called for a medical examination.

My emotions tangled into a knot — hope, dread, anxiety. Was this routine? Or a red flag? Had my case reached a critical point? I didn't know. I only knew I had to respond. I asked my doctor to write another detailed letter describing my condition — not just numbers and lab reports, but the story behind the struggle. I hoped they would see a person, not just a patient.

Then... silence.

Weeks passed. Every day I checked the mailbox with a mix of hope and dread. Nothing came. I knew that failed medicals often led to automatic rejection. And yet, no news could mean anything — an extended review, or just quiet dismissal. The silence was suffocating.

Meanwhile, Lee's visa had run its course. It had already been stretched past the 12-month limit on compassionate grounds. No further extension was possible. Our return tickets were also expiring. We faced a practical, painful decision: to return to Malaysia with no clear outcome.

So we packed.

On the Friday before our scheduled departure, we visited the immigration office in Sydney to formally withdraw my application and retrieve my passport.

The case officer came out to meet us, smiling in a way I couldn't quite read.

"Mr. Chin," he said, "you're quite well-known in our department. Your case is very unique. Everyone talks about it."

I couldn't tell whether that was a compliment or a warning. Was I memorable because my case was compelling — or because it was complicated?

I explained our situation: the expiring tickets, the visa, the silence. Our need to go. He listened, then surprised us with four options:

1. Stay and wait for the outcome.

2. Apply for another extension for Lee (though it wasn't guaranteed).
3. Withdraw and leave.
4. Leave with a re-entry visa — and keep the application alive.

The fourth option meant I could return to Malaysia temporarily, but with a special re-entry visa that would allow me to come back within six weeks — without cancelling my immigration application. It was a rare and generous concession. If I didn't return in time, the visa would expire and my case would be automatically closed.

The fourth option stunned me. I asked plainly: was there still a chance of approval?

He didn't answer directly. But his tone shifted — something in his eyes softened. "Your case is still under active consideration," he said.

Lee and I stepped aside.

She had already resigned. The bags were packed. The tickets were confirmed. We stood on the edge of goodbye. And yet — this offer, this thread of hope — it tugged at something deeper.

We made our decision.

I returned to the counter and said we'd take the fourth option.

The officer stamped my passport with a six-week return visa. "If you don't return within that time," he said, "your application will be cancelled."

Then came the part that still gives me chills.

"Actually," he added, "your file was scheduled to be transferred this morning to the Chatswood immigration office. If you had come even a little later, we wouldn't have been able to retrieve it. You got here just in time."

That moment stayed with me. A whisper of divine timing. A wink from above.

"You got here just in time!"

With no time to spare, we left the rest of our furniture behind and flew back to Malaysia the next morning.

Our arrival sparked joy. Family and friends were stunned by my recovery. It had been over a year, and many hadn't expected to see me like this — alive with new hair, walking, smiling. It was a celebration of survival.

For the next six weeks, I rested. I met old friends. I visited Kim's family. But inside, I was restless. Would I really return? Could I bear another round of uncertainty? Or had this all been a false hope?

One afternoon, Uncle George — who had visited us and had recently posted from Brisbane to work in Malaysia — offered some timely wisdom.

"This chance to return," he said gently, "even if it doesn't lead to approval, gives you control over your health and your future. That alone is worth everything."

His words sank in.

They didn't remove the uncertainty. But they gave it shape — a reason to try again. A reminder that not every answer is found in a letter or a visa, but in the courage to say yes to another chapter.

So I began to prepare — quietly, prayerfully — for what came next.

Not knowing the outcome. But trusting that perhaps, just perhaps, God was still writing this story.

Chapter 27

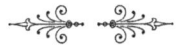

Grace at Every Turn

Six weeks passed swiftly. Despite the uncertainties and the heaviness in my heart, I chose to return to Australia, determined to await the outcome of my permanent residency application.

On December 1, 1988, I stepped once again onto Australian soil—this time with a deeper sense of hope and quiet resolve. I moved in with my cousin and his family, who had recently relocated from Wagga Wagga to Sydney. They had once stayed with us; now it was their turn to offer me shelter.

Just three days after arriving, I visited the immigration office to inquire about my case. To my disappointment, they informed me that the application was still being processed. No further updates were available. It puzzled me—six weeks had gone by, and it seemed nothing had changed. Perhaps they had paused the process during my absence, planning to resume only once I had returned.

In the second week, I needed to attend a follow-up appointment at the hospital. Not yet familiar with the new area, I intended to take the usual main road to the wharf and catch a ferry to the city. But that day, for no clear reason, I chose a smaller path and took a few unexpected turns. To my surprise, I stumbled upon a small church, hidden among the side streets of the neighbourhood: Manly Community AOG Church. Compelled by curiosity—or something greater—I walked in and found the pastor. I asked about their worship schedule and whether I could attend.

That Sunday, I joined their service. Unlike the previous churches I'd visited, this one was alive. The songs and sermons, even if not fully understood, were vibrant and uplifting. But what touched me most was the warmth of the congregation. After the service, people came up to greet me. One of the church leaders, Vaun Lessing, and his wife Linda, invited me to their home for lunch. Their kindness and sincere hospitality moved me deeply.

They welcomed me into their weekly Bible study group and patiently guided me through the scriptures. Slowly, I began to understand the stories and teachings. It wasn't just a gathering; it became a place of belonging. Though I was the only Chinese Malaysian there, I never felt out of place. They invited me to picnics, sports events, and gospel outreach activities. For the first time since arriving in Australia, I no longer felt alone.

Meanwhile, I had to plan for my future. I needed work, and I wanted to continue my education. The year-end holiday season made enrolment in college impossible right away, so I began by improving my English and exploring course options. I soon found a job as a kitchen assistant at a café on a popular tourist street in Manly. It was my first paid job in Australia. Though the work mostly involved cleaning and dishwashing, I also learned to prepare simple meals and began to understand the rhythm of a professional kitchen.

The café was owned by a Greek Australian family. The pay was modest, but I was grateful for the job and the opportunity to earn my own living. I worked hard and took pride in my responsibilities. One day, after finishing my morning shift, I felt so exhausted I went home to nap before my evening shift. I ended up sleeping until the next day and missed both shifts. We didn't have a phone at home, so I couldn't call in. When I returned on the third day, unsure if I still had a job, the boss surprisingly kept me on. Perhaps finding someone as hardworking and inexpensive as me wasn't easy.

Eventually, I realised that washing dishes wasn't my calling. With the college year approaching, I resigned and travelled to Adelaide to visit Kim. She had completed her 12th-grade exams with excellent results and had been accepted into the University of South Australia's accounting program. She was working hard over the summer to save for tuition.

After spending two weeks in Adelaide, I returned to Sydney to prepare for college. I decided to pursue a six-month catering course at Brookvale TAFE College—a practical choice that promised job opportunities upon completion. Although accounting remained my favourite subject, the time and language demands of a four-year program felt too daunting at that point.

I also landed a full-time job at Sizzler, a well-known restaurant chain conveniently located near my college. Balancing 38 hours of work with 20 hours of classes each week was challenging but fulfilling. A friend from church, Vaun, generously helped me buy a bicycle, even paying for it upfront when I didn't have enough cash.

The catering course was manageable. It resembled the culinary training I'd taken in Malaysia, covering nutrition, menu design, food presentation, cost calculation, kitchen operations, safety, and hygiene.

Yet, language remained a barrier. My English was still limited, and I struggled to fully connect with classmates. Cultural differences and jokes flew over my head. I felt out of place and insecure. One classmate, a widow in her 70s, (yes, you are still allowed to attend college at 70!) offered me a room to rent in her home, which was conveniently located near both my college and job. I accepted.

Shortly after I relocated, my cousin and his family were unexpectedly apprehended by immigration authorities and sent back to Malaysia. Was it merely a coincidence, or was it the grace of God? Had I not moved out, I could have been compelled to take over their lease. Being on my own, I undoubtedly wouldn't have been able to manage the exorbitant rent. I might have even faced the prospect of not having a place to stay!

Reflecting on it now, I believe it was grace. God had been making a way, even when in uncertainty, He was still writing my story—one step, one provision, one open door at a time.

Chapter 28

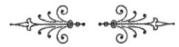

Seeds of Faith and a New Calling

Every Sunday, when I wasn't rostered to work, I made it a point to attend church. Unlike many others who could recall a specific day when they accepted Jesus as their Lord and Saviour, my journey was less defined—but no less profound.

I had begun reading the Bible, and slowly, through life experiences and quiet reflection, I found my heart drawn closer to faith. I came to understand that the Creator of the universe not only knew me but loved me. I realized that we are all sinners, falling short of God's glory, but through Jesus, we are welcomed back into the embrace of our Heavenly Father.

The church regularly held outdoor gospel outreach events, and over time, a growing number of Chinese international students began attending. Most of them spoke even less English than I did. But what drew them wasn't the language — it was the love, warmth, and genuine care of the brothers and sisters in Christ.

Like me, they had come to this foreign land with hopes of education and a better future, only to find themselves overwhelmed by homesickness, cultural differences, and the loneliness that often accompanies life far from home. In this unfamiliar world, the longing for unconditional love and belonging found its answer in the church.

This influx of Chinese students presented the church with a new challenge. Other than me, no one else could communicate in Chinese or share the gospel with them in their heart language. Recognizing this need, our pastor reached out to a dedicated brother named Doug. A carpenter by trade, Doug had once served as a missionary in India and had a heart for cross-cultural ministry. He accepted the call to shepherd this small but growing Chinese fellowship.

At first, these new friends attended the English services with everyone else. Despite not understanding much, they came faithfully and even invited others. Some travelled quite far, taking buses and ferries to reach the church. Yet within God's house, there was a unity that transcended language and culture. Week after week, new faces appeared, and the congregation began to witness God's incredible work among the Chinese community.

Eventually, the pastor recognized the need for a separate service tailored to the Chinese group. After singing hymns with the main congregation, we would head to a nearby community hall where Doug delivered a sermon. The church invited me to serve as his translator.

This was no easy task. My English was still limited, and my Chinese wasn't much better either. And having only recently come to faith, my understanding of doctrine was shallow. But Doug walked with me patiently. A day or two before each Sunday, he would go over his sermon with me, explaining everything clearly and giving me time to prepare. With the Holy Spirit's help, I managed to translate.

Doing this stirred a hunger in me to learn more. I began to read the Bible more deeply and consistently. I wanted to understand — not just to translate the message, but to live it. I knew God had saved me, and now I was seeing how He could also use me.

As the fellowship grew, Doug started a small group Bible study for the Chinese believers. He taught them to pray, study Scripture, and serve. Despite having a full-time job, Doug poured his heart into the ministry. His example taught us that serving the Lord requires no title, only love and willingness. Through his ministry, many of the students came to faith, and some began to take part in service themselves.

For me, this period marked a transformation. I wasn't just recovering physically or building a life in a foreign land — I was finding purpose. I began to dream of studying at a Bible college someday, to learn more and serve others with greater understanding.

And then, in November 1991, on a Sunday that will forever remain etched in my memory, I was baptized.

Not in a grand ceremony, not with fanfare or applause. But with deep gratitude, quiet joy, and a heart fully surrendered to the One who had never stopped pursuing me.

Chapter 29

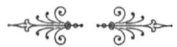

Trials of Delay and the Faith to Persevere

I continued to check regularly with the immigration office about the progress of my permanent residency application, but the answer never changed: still in progress. After several months of silence, I finally received an update—but it wasn't the news I had hoped for. During the character check phase, the Malaysian government reported that I had a criminal record. The immigration officers couldn't give me any details, only that the report from Malaysia flagged my name.

I was stunned. What record? I had never committed any crime! Desperate to understand, I asked to see the report, but the officers explained that it was classified as a confidential government document. I wasn't even allowed to see what I was being accused of. The injustice of the situation weighed heavily on me. How could I defend myself against a charge I couldn't see?

I did my best to be transparent. I confessed that I had once been involved in a minor car accident and had previously lost my Malaysian identification card. Could either of those incidents have somehow been misrepresented or misfiled? Still, my explanation wasn't enough. The immigration office had already sent multiple telegrams to the Australian Embassy in Malaysia requesting clarification, but the Malaysian government had yet to respond. My application couldn't proceed without that reply.

It was frustrating. I knew my application had passed the more difficult hurdles, including the medical review. If they had intended to reject me on health grounds, they would have done it earlier. This character check seemed to be the final barrier. And now my future hung in limbo because of a mystery accusation I couldn't refute. I contacted my father and asked him to help investigate and apply for a good character certificate on my behalf in Malaysia.

Meanwhile, I continued to work and build my life. After several months at Sizzler, I was promoted from kitchen hand to cook. It was a big step up. I learned how to marinate meats, manage portions, store food correctly, and cook steaks to each customer's preference. The pressure in the kitchen could be intense—especially during busy periods—but I took pride in the work. Even when I missed the relative ease of dishwashing, I knew I was growing.

After completing my catering course, I moved on from Sizzler and took a more favourable position as the sole cook at a café inside the Grace Brothers department store. The hours were better—9 a.m. to 3 p.m.—and the pay was higher. My role included preparing a selection of simple yet well-loved dishes: fried rice packed with vegetables and egg, wok-tossed noodles glistening with soy sauce, crispy chicken nuggets, and tangy lemon chicken that quickly became a lunchtime favourite.

Over time, I was even given the opportunity to introduce a few new items to the menu—dishes inspired by home, like stir-fried vegetables with tofu, sweet and sour fish, and a milder version of curry chicken tailored to curious Aussie palates. The list gradually grew, adding subtle flavours of Asian home cooking to an otherwise basic menu. Though the offerings remained modest, I took pride in every plate I served. Watching customers enjoy the food—and even return for more—gave me a quiet sense of fulfilment. Best of all, Sundays were free, allowing me to attend church more regularly and settle into a new rhythm of life.

Still, 30 hours a week left too much unstructured time. I looked for additional work and soon found a casual job washing cars at the Manly Children's Hospital. They had ten institutional vehicles that needed cleaning each week, and I could fit in the 10-hour job around my café schedule.

Yet even that wasn't enough to fill my evenings. I prayed, and not long after, God opened another door. I landed a part-time position at a high-end seafood restaurant in Manly. I worked three evenings a week and most Saturdays. Occasionally, I covered Sunday shifts. My responsibility was grilling the fish—a job I enjoyed. The atmosphere was friendly and respectful, and I even admired the wait staff for earning more in tips than their hourly wage.

Altogether, I was working nearly 60 hours a week. Strangely, I never felt overly tired. Perhaps it was the motivation of earning money, or maybe God was strengthening me for that season. In my free time, I wrote letters to Kim and my family, read the Bible, and kept up with my hospital check-ups every two months. GVHD was still present, but well-managed.

Life felt full and stable. And yet, always in the background, the immigration application loomed—unresolved and unknown. The weight of uncertainty never fully lifted. But amid it all, I chose to keep believing that God, who had brought me this far, would carry me through.

Chapter 30

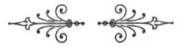

Detours of Disappointment and a New Season of Growth

In January 1990, I made plans to return to Malaysia to celebrate the Lunar New Year with my family—a long-awaited reunion after more than two years apart. The trip also coincided with Kim's third sister's wedding, and it had been a full year since I had last seen Kim. Both of us had been leading busy lives—I was working nearly 60 hours a week across multiple jobs, and Kim was balancing her university studies with part-time work. Our longing for each other had grown deeper, and the idea of reuniting brought immense anticipation.

However, there was one major hurdle: getting the time off work. I had just started a new position at the Grace Brothers café and knew it would be difficult to secure leave so soon. But the yearning to return home and see my loved ones was too strong. I made the difficult decision to resign from the job, believing I would find another one upon my return to Australia.

After booking my flight, I went to the immigration office to request a return visa. To my shock, they denied it. Unlike the previous time, when I was granted a visa to return after visiting Malaysia, this time they said my application was still under review and leaving the country could jeopardize it.

The news hit me hard. I had already resigned from work and now couldn't return home either. It felt like I was stuck in limbo—unable to go back, unable to move forward. I blamed myself for not thinking it through more carefully. Fortunately, I still had my part-time jobs at the seafood restaurant and the hospital car wash. But I urgently needed full-time work.

Despite applying at various places and attending interviews, my lack of formal experience hindered my chances. Then one day, while washing cars at the hospital, my boss approached me with an offer: a full-time kitchen assistant position had opened in the hospital kitchen. Though it wasn't my dream job, I needed the income and accepted it.

The workweek was standard—Monday to Friday, 9 a.m. to 5:30 p.m. I was the only male in a kitchen staffed by women from Yugoslavia. Despite the cultural and language differences, I felt surprisingly comfortable. The work was simple and repetitive, but the team was kind and welcoming. After the lunchtime rush, there wasn't much left to do, so I brought books and magazines to keep myself occupied.

I continued working evenings at the seafood restaurant. As for the car washing job, I handed it over to Minqi, a cleaner who worked at the hospital. Through that connection, we became friends.

Around that time, my landlady asked me to move out because my rent payments had exceeded the income limit permitted under her pension benefits.

Thankfully, Minqi informed me about the hospital's dormitory accommodation for staff. The rent was just $35 a week, less than half of what I was previously paying. Even better, it was located directly above my workplace—a two-minute walk to the hospital kitchen, and just a street away from the seafood restaurant and Manly Beach.

But the true blessing of the new dormitory wasn't just the convenience or affordability—it was the people. I shared the space with two devoted Christians: Minqi and Michael, an Australian with a powerful testimony of transformation through Christ. Together, we cooked, shared meals, prayed, and studied the Bible. My faith began to grow rapidly during this period. Their example of godly living and heartfelt devotion had a profound impact on me.

Although it had begun with disappointment, this unexpected detour became one of the most enriching and formative seasons of my life. God had closed one door, but He opened another—one that led not just to provision, but to deeper spiritual growth and renewed purpose.

Looking back now, I can see it clearly—it was grace. At the time, it felt like failure and setback. The denial of my return visa seemed like a closed door, a missed opportunity. But now I understand: had that door not closed, I would have stayed in the comfort of my café job, missed the offer at the hospital, and never crossed paths with Minqi. Without that connection, I wouldn't have moved into the dormitory—and I may never have encountered the kind of spiritual community that caused my faith to truly flourish.

Each disappointment had been a redirection. What felt like disruption was actually design. Thread by thread, God was weaving something far greater than I could see. Was it fate? Coincidence? Or was it the quiet hand of God, faithfully guiding my every step, working behind the scenes of my story, even when I didn't know I was being led?

Chapter 31

Waiting for a Breakthrough

Many months had gone by, and I was still without any updates from the immigration office. During that period, I felt truly lost. I had no other alternatives except prayer. The prayers I offered during those days were arguably the most sincere and fervent of my life. Yet God did not seem to answer or intervene.

My application remained in limbo because of an ambiguous and unexplained record. The immigration office kept sending telegrams to the Australian Embassy in Malaysia, and the embassy continued to press the Malaysian government for clarification. But the Malaysian authorities remained unresponsive. It was frustrating beyond words. If I had a criminal record, why couldn't they just disclose it? Or had they made a mistake and were unwilling to admit it? I felt like I was being punished for something I didn't do.

Finally, I received a letter from my father. He informed me that he had submitted applications to the Ministry of Home Affairs, the Ministry of Foreign Affairs, and the Police Headquarters in Malaysia for a Certificate of Good Character on my behalf. The anticipated waiting period for a response was three months. That seemed like forever, but it was at least a flicker of hope. I entrusted the matter to the Lord, hoping for clarity and truth to prevail. Though I knew I was innocent, I continued to pray with deep urgency.

Exactly three months later, I received another letter from my father. My hands trembled as I opened it. Inside was an official document from the Malaysian Ministry of Foreign Affairs, dated September 5, 1990. It read: "The Malaysian government certifies that the Malaysian citizen, Chin Tian Tat, holder of Malaysian Passport No. A2258746, has no criminal record in Malaysia." I hadn't even finished reading before tears of relief filled my eyes. Finally—finally! I rushed to submit it to the immigration office, praying this would lead to a swift decision.

But two more months passed. Still no word.

I couldn't believe it. Why were they still delaying? The stress of not knowing gnawed at me daily. I kept working at the hospital kitchen and continued my evening shifts at the seafood restaurant. But with the hospital closing for three weeks over the Christmas period, I took the opportunity to travel to Adelaide and visit Kim. It had been two years since we last saw each other.

This time, I could afford a plane ticket, thanks to the launch of a new budget airline, Compass. It was a short trip, but so meaningful. I met Kim's university friends, helped out at her workplace—a roast chicken shop—and spent precious time together. We talked about the future. During a New Year's service at Paradise AOG Church, the pastor delivered a message about unity in relationships. That message deeply moved both of us. We committed to staying united in every decision, no matter where life led us.

After the New Year, I prepared to return to Sydney. Unfortunately, the budget airline had gone out of business. Plane tickets had skyrocketed in price, and I couldn't find an affordable seat. I eventually booked a train ticket—a 24-hour journey that tested every ounce of patience I had.

Returning to Sydney, I resumed work. Then, at the end of January 1991, a letter from the immigration office finally arrived. My heart pounded. Was this it? Was my application approved?

It wasn't. Instead, they requested another medical report and an updated letter from my doctor outlining my current health condition and whether I still needed treatment in Australia. By this time, several officers had changed on my case, and my file had likely been reviewed afresh. I had to start again—submitting updated documents and waiting once more.

Despite the setback, I tried to stay hopeful. After all I had endured, I couldn't afford to give up now. God had not brought me this far to leave me. The breakthrough, I believed, was still coming.

Chapter 32

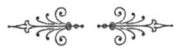

The Proposal and a Promise

After submitting my latest medical report, months passed once again, and the immigration office remained silent. I couldn't understand what was taking so long. Was my case truly that complex, or was their system simply inefficient? Despite continued prayers, God's timing remained a mystery. Every day felt like walking through fog, unsure of what lay ahead.

Finally, in May, a letter from the immigration office arrived. My heart surged with hope—this had to be the answer I'd waited for. But upon opening it, I discovered it was yet another request: I needed to undergo another medical examination because the last one had expired. My disappointment was overwhelming. Were they just looking for more reasons to delay or reject my application? Regardless, I complied and returned to the health department for another check-up.

That July, during her university break, Kim came to visit me in Sydney. After all the times I'd travelled to see her, it was her turn. I didn't want her enduring another exhausting 17-hour bus ride, so I bought her a round-trip plane ticket. It was expensive, but worth every cent. I arranged for her to stay with a gracious Korean couple from my church, and proudly introduced her to my friends and colleagues.

Our time together was magical. We toured Sydney, visited iconic beaches, strolled through Chinatown, and even spent a romantic evening admiring the harbor from a ferry. We rented a car and drove through the Blue Mountains and all the way to Canberra. The highlight of our trip was experiencing Australia's snow-capped mountains. That holiday became a treasured chapter in our journey together—one filled with laughter, adventure, and memories to last a lifetime.

But even amid the joy, our conversations turned serious. We discussed marriage, but I couldn't shake the feeling that I might be burdening Kim. Though my GVHD was under control, it was still a shadow in our lives. The doctors believed it would eventually fade, but there were no guarantees. I had also been told that my chances of having children were zero. Our career paths seemed worlds apart—Kim was becoming an accountant, and I was working long hours in restaurant kitchens.

Although social status wasn't a major issue in Australia, I couldn't help worrying about what Kim might be sacrificing by staying with me. But her love remained steadfast. She never wavered, proving time and again that real love was not about what I had, but who I was.

We talked about where we might live if I received residency. I wanted to stay in Manly, where my church and community were. Kim preferred Adelaide—the quieter pace, the lower cost of living, the chance to build something new. A house in Adelaide costs half what it would in Sydney. But Sydney offered more job opportunities. Our future was filled with unknowns, but we were determined to face them together.

After ten wonderful days, Kim returned to Adelaide to finish her final semester. My medical exam had already been completed over two months prior, and still, no word from immigration. Growing impatient, I requested to view my immigration file. On August 1, I received it. Some documents were redacted, but I could finally trace the entire journey of my application.

I discovered that, at one point, the health department had recommended my rejection due to medical concerns. But the immigration office had considered waiving that requirement subject to my character check. Then the confusion with the Malaysian government's erroneous records caused further delays. Even after submitting proof of my good character, the final note in my file showed yet another request for a medical update. It was disheartening.

Still, life moved on. On my 27th birthday, after finishing a night shift, I called Kim and proposed. There were no roses, no candles, no ring. Just a phone call—and she said yes. We kept the news private. Kim still had half a year of studies to complete, and I still had no certainty about my immigration status. I felt I had nothing material to offer her.

Around that time, Kim's boss, Peter, asked about our plans. Hearing our story, he made an extraordinary offer. If we were willing to settle in Adelaide, he would sell us half of his restaurant business. He respected Kim's integrity and dedication and wanted to semi-retire. This offer, completely unexpected, lifted a huge weight off our shoulders. It was a sign that maybe, just maybe, things were beginning to fall into place.

The future still held many uncertainties, but we had taken the first step toward building it together. With faith in God and each other, we had made a promise—and that was more than enough to carry us forward.

Chapter 33

God's Perfect Timing

On the fateful date of September 16, 1991, the long-awaited letter from the immigration office finally arrived. The moment I held the envelope in my hands, waves of emotion washed over me. Could this finally be the end of the years-long uncertainty? I hesitated, torn between hope and fear, even wishing someone else could open it for me. The possibility of rejection weighed heavily on my heart.

Summoning all my courage, I opened the envelope. My eyes darted to the first line. "I am pleased to inform you that your immigration application has been approved." Time seemed to pause. I read it again to make sure. Tears welled in my eyes—tears of joy, relief, disbelief. It had been a gruelling, three-year wait filled with rejections, appeals, unknowns, and prayer. But now, I could finally breathe. I had been granted permanent residency in Australia. I was home.

Australia was more than just a place to me. It had saved my father's life, offered me a life-saving bone marrow transplant, and now welcomed me to stay. It felt like divine grace—a country that gave without expecting, a second chance at life. Mark 10:27 (NIV) echoed in my heart: "With man this is impossible, but not with God; all things are possible with God."

My journey made that verse real. Immigration officers had discouraged me from applying. They said the chances were zero. But God had a different plan. His miracles often come wrapped in impossible circumstances. And His timing? Impeccable.

At times, I questioned why God delayed my approval. Why allow the false criminal record from Malaysia? Why the silence from the government? But looking back, I saw the purpose. Had my application been approved in 1989, I likely would have rushed to Adelaide, moved in with Kim, and taken steps that could have disrupted both her studies and my spiritual growth. The detour in Manly had led me to faith, to mentorship, and to a church that nurtured me. Kim was able to complete her studies without distraction. God had orchestrated everything.

What seemed like a delay was, in truth, God's protection—steering me away from paths I wasn't ready for, and into places where I would grow, heal, and be prepared for what lay ahead.

In His delay, I grew. Spiritually. Emotionally. In character. I learned to wait, to pray, to trust. My relationship with God deepened. He placed people in my life, jobs to sustain me, and communities to support me. The pieces all fit—eventually.

Now, with my residency secured, Kim and I could plan a future without fear. Her scholarship terms required her to leave the country after graduation, but now, there was hope she could stay. We were on the verge of building a life together.

I remembered when a Christian friend first shared the gospel with me. I challenged God then, demanding healing as proof of His power. He didn't heal me on my terms, but He never left me. Isaiah 55:8-9 (NIV) came alive: "For my thoughts are not your thoughts, neither are your ways my ways..."

God had chosen not to give me what I wanted, when I wanted it. Instead, He gave me something far greater—a transformed life. His delay was not denial; it was divine preparation. His thoughts, His ways, were truly higher than mine.

As I closed the letter and looked ahead, I was filled with gratitude. The waiting was over. A new chapter had begun. And God had written every line.

Chapter 34

A Covenant of Love

Part 1: A Love Preserved by Grace

In November 1991, a significant milestone marked Kim's completion of her undergraduate studies in accounting. The accomplishment ignited a deep conversation between us, leading us to earnestly contemplate the idea of getting married right after her graduation.

Excitedly, Kim shared this plan with her sister, Doris, and Doris's husband, Trevor. However, their response was one of surprise, expressing concern about the eagerness to marry immediately. Their advice was rooted in the suggestion that Kim should prioritize the establishment of her career, considering that she had just graduated.

In the midst of our considerations, we didn't seek marital counselling, driven partly by the constraints of time and a lack of understanding of the potential benefits of Christian marriage counselling. Nevertheless, the echoes of the New Year's message at the church lingered in our minds, emphasizing the importance of unity and oneness in our considerations and decisions.

Reflecting on our eight years of dating history, which was marked by periods of separation and reunification, as well as navigating through numerous challenges, the stability of our relationship emerged as a testament to God's preservation, blessing, and grace. The decision not to be apart any longer was rooted in our deep awareness of the love we shared, propelling us to embark on the exciting journey of love together.

As January 1992 unfolded, we went back to Malaysia for vacation and to prepare for the celebration of the Lunar New Year with our respective families and with the potential intention of getting married.

Remarkably, this marked five years since I had spent the Lunar New Year with my family! However, time constraints hindered us from adequately preparing our families for our imminent marriage plans. Nonetheless, our intention was to register our marriage first and plan a wedding a year later. After our vacations, the plan was to return to Sydney together before making the move to Adelaide, symbolizing the commencement of the next chapter in our lives.

After three long years away, I finally returned home again. And this time, I carried with me a new identity – that of an Australian permanent resident. The moment I set foot in the airport and laid eyes on my parents, an overwhelming sense of joy and nostalgia enveloped me. Without hesitation, I embraced them, realizing that the last time we shared such a heartfelt hug, I was likely still a child. Hugging wasn't a familiar gesture in our family, so my embrace may have taken them by surprise, but I knew it brought them comfort. This gesture was my way of expressing gratitude, love, and the deep longing I had felt for them.

As I stepped into the comforting embrace of my home, a wave of profound emotion swept over me. The longing for the warmth and charm of my home, the familiar sounds of family, and, above all, the delightful aroma of my mom's signature dishes, filled my heart. The collective joy within everyone went beyond the relief of my safe return; it was tinged with amazement at the miraculous attainment of Australian permanent residency. Their happiness and reassurance were grounded in the realization that I no longer had to grapple with uncertainties about my health and future. Australia, in their eyes, held the promise of providing me with a healthy and purposeful life.

Part 2: A Journey Blessed by Promise

A week later, Kim returned to Malaysia from Adelaide, and naturally, I was at the airport to welcome her. Despite her brother being present for the welcome, she chose me to accompany her home. On the journey back, laughter filled the car as we shared silly anecdotes, and in those moments, we couldn't help but reminisce about the bittersweet journey we once took together from my home to the airport when she bid me farewell to my uncertainty. Little did we imagine that today, we would be sitting side by side in the car, joyfully heading home from the airport together. The excitement and gratitude we felt were palpable, and we acknowledged that God's greatness had transformed all our hardships into blessings.

With the blessings and approval of both our families, we proceeded to register our marriage at the Marriage Registry on February 26, 1992. This legal recognition marked the beginning of our journey as a married couple. However, while we were officially married in the eyes of the law, the absence of a traditional wedding ceremony left our family and relatives with the sense that our union wasn't fully formalized. Despite the legal recognition, we decided to delay the celebrations and rituals until the following year when we could host a grand wedding ceremony.

Following the Lunar New Year festivities, Kim and I returned to Sydney as Mr and Mrs Chin, officially united in matrimony. Eager to commence the next chapter of our lives, I promptly contacted Kim's boss, Peter to confirm the plans he had previously discussed. Subsequently, I took the time to bid farewell to my cherished friends, church community, and colleagues in Manly. With the next destination set, we embarked on a journey from Sydney to Adelaide, navigating the distance in a rented car, filled with anticipation for the adventures that awaited us.

We passed through Melbourne without stopping and, instead, stayed overnight in a small city, Geelong. From there, we travelled along the Great Ocean Road to Mt Gambier, where we spent another night, before hastily returning to Adelaide! Although this three-day, extremely short journey served as our honeymoon, we later regretted not taking the opportunity to explore more during this period before our working life began. Perhaps our eagerness to settle down quickly played a role! We recognized the missed opportunities to immerse ourselves in new experiences and create lasting memories during those carefree days.

Despite the short honeymoon, those three days held a unique significance for us because they represented the closure of a chapter marked by physical separations. This was a pivotal moment, aligning with the promises of unity and oneness that God had spoken into our lives. Little did we anticipate that our love, having weathered countless trials and tribulations, would not only endure but also continue to flourish vibrantly.

In the midst of the scenic landscapes and shared moments, there were times when we questioned the reality of our journey. The symbolism of the frog prince finally marrying his beautiful princess felt surreal and magical. The journey had transformed from the trials of separation to the celebration of unity, and we eagerly embraced the new chapter that awaited us as a married couple.

We firmly believe that we will have a bright future, just as Romans 8:31 (NIV) declares, "If God is for us, who can be against us?" We also hold onto the promise from Jeremiah 29:11, (NLT): "For I know the plans I have for you, declares the Lord, plans for welfare and not for evil, to give you a future and a hope." We trust that these are God's promises for us, and we believe He will continue to bless us abundantly, enabling us to be a blessing to others.

Initially, we stayed temporarily at Doris and Trevor's home and soon rented an apartment next door. We started attending Paradise Assembly of God Church, now known as Futures Church. This was the church Kim joined when she first arrived, and it is also the largest church in South Australia, with thousands of people attending worship services every week. We were drawn to the worship atmosphere and the messages of this church, deciding to make it our spiritual home.

We also joined a home life group within the church, meeting every two weeks and led by a devoted couple – the husband is a dentist, and the wife is a homemaker, with both daughters already married. They were friendly and compassionate, and the members of their group consisted of international students and immigrants from Asian countries. The gatherings, usually attended by twenty to thirty people, created a sense of unity and connection among members who shared a similar background. The fellowship and mutual support within this community enriched our spiritual journey, creating a sense of belonging and purpose that strengthened our faith and bonds with fellow believers.

Chapter 35

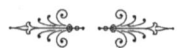

The Wilderness Between The Promises

During a discussion with Peter, he surprised us by proposing an unexpected alternative to our original plan. Instead of what we had in mind, he suggested venturing into the business of selling chicken—within a seafood shop owned by one of his friends in town. Peter believed that this unusual pairing would offer customers the convenience of buying both seafood and chicken in one place. He guaranteed a steady chicken supply from his wholesale meat store, and I was tasked with managing the sales in the shop.

Given my current unemployment, I saw it as a chance to explore something new and potentially rewarding. The idea of navigating the ins and outs of a fish-and-chicken retail venture felt both practical and intriguing. We agreed to move forward, hopeful that this hybrid model would offer customers a unique shopping experience. Partnering with Peter's friend marked the start of a new chapter—one filled with unexpected challenges, valuable lessons, and more than a few surprises.

Without hesitation, we plunged into the chicken-selling venture at Peter's friend's shop. Leaning on my past experiences, I had a degree of familiarity with this type of small business, having assisted my parents in selling chicken and duck meat at the market during my youth. Meanwhile, Kim, in her pursuit of opportunities in the accounting field, dedicated her evenings to working at a restaurant and spent her free time supporting me in the shop.

We persevered in this endeavour for a span of three months. Despite observing some progress in the business, the profitability fell short of our expectations. The earnings generated proved insufficient to cover my wages, compelling us to make the challenging decision to close the shop. This brief yet intense experience provided us with valuable insights into the complexities of running a retail operation, imparting lessons that would undoubtedly prove beneficial in our future endeavours.

Subsequently, Peter proposed that I join the team at his wholesale meat store, a business catering to the meat supply needs of the majority of Chinese restaurants in Adelaide. He highlighted that the business operations were currently suboptimal, and due to his time constraints, he inquired if I would consider taking on the responsibility. In essence, my responsibilities would include following up with and visiting all customers, enhancing service delivery, managing debt collection, and expanding the customer base. I openly acknowledged to him that I lacked experience in this particular field but expressed my willingness to embrace the challenge and give it a try.

I accepted this challenge and began visiting and getting to know all the customers, building good relationships with them, and trying to promote additional products. The competition in the meat wholesale market was fierce, and to attract and please some customers, everyone was willing to lower prices. My weekly schedule involved spending two days meeting with customers outside and three days manning the store counter, catering to the public's demand for meat.

Regrettably, I found little enjoyment in this job, recognizing its limited prospects. My presence here was only a temporary measure as I explored alternative opportunities. Additionally, I frequently fell ill, attributing it to the less-than-ideal hygiene conditions in the shop. Handling various types of meat daily and the constant transitions in and out of the cold room likely contributed to my health issues.

Moreover, Kim and I were dissatisfied with our work schedules, which provided us with little opportunities for meaningful conversations and shared activities. Given my early morning start, upon returning home in the evening, Kim would be on her way to the restaurant for her shift. Even after finishing her work and reaching home, it was often quite late, sometimes even later. I would already be in a deep slumber, gearing up for an early wake-up the following day for work.

Hoping to pursue my interest in accounting and return to college, I decided to explore an alternative route rather than undertaking a foundation or pre-tertiary bridging course. I opted for the Special Tertiary Admissions Test, designed for adults without proper qualifications but considering a return to education. Unfortunately, I did not pass the test. Concurrently, I actively sought potential opportunities for small businesses, but none turned out to be a perfect fit. Kim faced her own challenges in securing the job she aspired to, with even volunteer work opportunities proving elusive.

Chapter 36

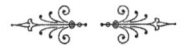

A Promise in the Wilderness

During this period of discouragement, Australia was grappling with a prolonged economic downturn. Job scarcity and a lack of opportunities burdened our spirits. Despite our faith in God's provision and the promises of Romans 8:31 and Jeremiah 29:11, doubts began to creep in. Was Adelaide really where we were meant to be? Had we misunderstood God's leading? Should we consider relocating to Sydney, or perhaps return to Malaysia, where job prospects were far more promising?

After much prayer, we set a deadline in our hearts—we told God that if nothing happened by a certain date, we would pack up and return to Malaysia. But God, in His mercy, responded. One morning, during my quiet time, my eyes were drawn to Genesis 26:1–6: (NIV)

"1 Now there was a famine in the land—besides the previous famine in Abraham's time—and Isaac went to Abimelek king of the Philistines in Gerar. 2 The Lord appeared to Isaac and said, 'Do not go down to Egypt; live in the land where I tell you to live. 3 Stay in this land for a while, and I will be with you and will bless you. For to you and your descendants I will give all these lands and will confirm the oath I swore to your father Abraham. 4 I will make your descendants as numerous as the stars in the sky and will give them all these lands, and through your offspring all nations on earth will be blessed, 5 because Abraham obeyed me and did everything I required of him, keeping my commands, my decrees and my instructions.' 6 So Isaac stayed in Gerar."

As I immersed myself in this passage, it felt as if these words were coming alive, speaking directly to me. Even though I had encountered this story numerous times before, this experience carried a distinct and touching resonance. The words, spoken by God to Isaac thousands of years ago, somehow felt as though He was addressing me in the present moment. Without delay, I shared and reflected on this profound revelation with Kim.

Malaysia was like Egypt—prosperous and full of promise. But God was asking us to stay in our own Gerar—Adelaide. He reminded us that His presence and blessings were not dependent on external circumstances but on obedience and trust. Though we were sceptical about the promise of numerous descendants—given my infertility diagnosis—we clung to the assurance that He would bless us in this land.

Bolstered by this conviction, we reaffirmed our decision to stay. Still, practical challenges remained. I decided to resign from the wholesale meat job, which was taking a toll on my health and our marriage. When I informed Peter, he inquired about my plans. I mentioned my intention to look for another job or explore business opportunities. Once again, Peter expressed interest in offering me half of the restaurant's shares and asked if I was still interested. Despite suggesting a trial period of working in the restaurant before deciding, he disagreed, emphasizing his desire for us to have shares, allowing us to concentrate more on working and managing the business.

Peter initially pursued a career as an electrical engineer but transitioned to running this business immediately after completing university, taking on the role of head chef. His wife, also a university graduate, joined him in managing the business after their marriage. Despite not following paths related to their studies, they found success together in the restaurant industry. Therefore, even if Kim didn't work as an accountant, she could still have a fulfilling life in the restaurant business.

Though daunting, we saw this as God's open door. With financial help from my parents, we bought into the business. Peter, who had run the restaurant successfully with his wife Wendy for years, began training me. The workload was immense: the restaurant operated seven days a week, from 10 a.m. to 10 p.m., often with lingering customers late into the night. Peter cooked for 160 guests with the efficiency of three chefs—an astonishing feat.

Operating seven days a week, our routine incorporated a designated day off every Wednesday to participate in the church's family group. On these days, I assumed the responsibility of opening and closing the restaurant, handling various administrative tasks, and managing miscellaneous aspects. Peter's presence was only mandatory during peak hours, allowing him some respite. My specific duties encompassed the intricate tasks of deep frying and preparing all meats and vegetables.

Despite the demanding nature of our roles, Kim and I found ourselves profoundly grateful for this arrangement. Beyond the extensive working hours, the true blessing lay in having a full day off, providing us with the invaluable opportunity to spend more quality time together.

Living in the eastern suburbs had been a dream, and by God's grace, that too became reality. Mark, a friend, urged us to view a run-down house near the restaurant. Though we initially dismissed it, its location and potential made us reconsider. With minimal renovation, it became our home.

THE DIVINE COINCIDENCE

The Lunar New Year marks the most vibrant day for Chinese restaurants in Australia. These establishments often arrange lion dance troupes and martial arts performances to draw in customers, creating a lively and celebratory atmosphere. Even for those who are not of Chinese descent, there is keen anticipation for this day to witness the spectacular performances.

Chapter 37

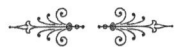

The Wedding We Almost Didn't Have

After the Lunar New Year festivities—the crescendo of color, noise, and tradition—when the lion dances rested and the restaurant lights dimmed, a quieter yearning stirred in our hearts. With business slowing down and time briefly on our side, Kim and I journeyed back to Malaysia, hearts full of anticipation, to celebrate the wedding ceremony we had always dreamed of. Though legally married, we longed to place our union before God and family in a sacred setting, inviting our loved ones—especially those yet to know Christ—to witness the testimony of God's guiding hand in our lives.

Our first hope was to hold the ceremony at Kim's sister's church. But our request was gently declined. Since we were already legally married, the church was unable to host a traditional wedding. The pastor, however, kindly offered to conduct a blessing service in a garden or alternative venue. We were grateful for her willingness, yet our hearts ached.

We had long envisioned standing before the altar—within the church's sacred walls—sanctifying our covenant in the presence of God and family.

More than just a ceremony, it would have been a quiet invitation for our loved ones, especially those who had never stepped inside a church, to encounter God's love through our story.

Undeterred, we sought another church. A kind pastor, moved by our story and sincerity, agreed to conduct the ceremony. But once again, the doors didn't open—the date we'd chosen was already booked, and alternative arrangements were nearly impossible given the short notice. Disappointment crept in, like a shadow in the late afternoon sun. It seemed the church wedding we envisioned—the one rooted in gratitude and glory—might not come to pass.

And so, we pivoted. We planned a traditional Chinese wedding instead, letting go of what could not be, and embracing what was in our hands. The days flew by in a blur of red invitations, silk garments, laughter, and hurried photographs. On February 28, 1993, in the presence of hundreds—most of whom were our parents' guests—we tied the knot once more.

The celebration was, in its own way, grand. We borrowed my dad's brother-in-law's brand-new Mercedes as our bridal car—a small nod to luxury on a modest budget. My younger brother, a talented pastry chef, lovingly crafted our wedding cake. Our home buzzed with joy as a ten-course banquet unfolded for nearly three hundred guests. Though our own circle was modest, the love in the room swelled large.

Kim's parents, too, hosted a banquet at a restaurant a week before the wedding, a testament to their support and joy.

And though there was no sanctuary aisle or stained-glass backdrop, the sacredness of that day lived in our hearts. The vows may not have been spoken in church, but they were written with ink eternal—in the sight of God who had brought us through valleys and deserts, to this promise fulfilled.

There was no extravagant honeymoon. Just two weeks later, we returned to Adelaide. Our 'getaway' was not a sun-soaked island but a dusty house in need of love and labour. We scrubbed floors, patched walls, and pieced together our first home with second-hand furniture and grateful hearts. Each improvement, however small, felt like a step forward—a blessing received, a prayer answered.

The house wasn't perfect. But it was ours. Nestled in the eastern suburbs we had once only dreamed of, it stood as a monument to faith tested and love persevering. Over the next two years, we painted, repaired, and built not just a home, but a life.

This chapter of our journey was defined not by glamour, but by grit; not by ceremony, but by covenant. And in that sacred wilderness between the promises, we found something more enduring than gold, more precious than tradition—we found the abiding presence of God, ever faithful, ever near.

Chapter 38

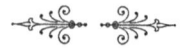

Held by a Whispered Promise

Part 1: When Hope Meets the Impossible

Every winter, my weakened immune system left me vulnerable to infection. What began as sniffles and fatigue often ended in a hospital bed, IVs dripping into my veins. One chilly evening, as Kim and I headed to our family group meeting, I felt that familiar heaviness in my body. Something was coming. At the meeting, our group gathered around me in prayer, two visiting brothers among them. One of them, with conviction in his voice, said God had told him my immune system was being strengthened—that I was already healed.

"Amen," I whispered, clinging to the words like a life raft.

That night, my fever faded. By morning, I was completely well. From that day on, illness rarely visited me, and even when it did, it was mild—gone in a day or two. No hospital. No antibiotics. Just grace. Sometimes I'd joke about missing the rest and "luxury" of hospital beds, but I never stopped thanking Jesus for His healing hand.

In our family group, many wives were expecting children. Their glowing anticipation stirred something deep within us. We dreamed of a child—of laughter echoing in our home. But we also carried the ache of what we believed was impossible.

Still, we prayed. We reminded ourselves that nothing was too hard for God. As Jesus said in Luke 18:27, (NIV) "What is impossible with man is possible with God."

We held on to His promises—like stars scattered across the sky, glimmering reminders of what had once been spoken in moments of intimacy with God. We remembered prophetic words spoken over us, the quiet confirmations that came in prayer, and the scriptures that had jumped from the page straight into our hearts. These promises weren't vague hopes—they were deeply personal, echoing dreams we'd barely dared to whisper aloud. In our midnight prayers and morning devotions, these promises had taken root, forming an invisible thread pulling us forward through disappointment and doubt.

Though circumstances seemed barren, these heavenly promises kept our faith alive, reminding us that God writes stories with impossible ink. Not long ago, God had spoken of descendants, of blessings flowing through our family. Could He still mean that? Did He still intend to do the miraculous?

To be sure, I went for another fertility test. The results were no surprise: The doctor was kind but honest—there was no improvement. Seven years since the operation. Seven years of hoping. The door remained closed. Even before the transplant, I'd been told there would be no freezing, no backup plan—no second chance.

I remember sitting across from the doctor, trying to absorb what those words really meant. It was more than just a clinical fact—it was the quiet death of a dream. There would be no sperm saved, no future path back to natural conception. Kim and I had clung to hope in silence, but hearing those words felt like a cold door swinging shut.

We left the clinic in a heavy stillness, not quite ready to talk. Inwardly, I wrestled with waves of guilt and helplessness, feeling like I had failed her. She, ever gracious, simply reached for my hand. We walked together that day—not toward answers, but toward surrender. That was the beginning of our journey through impossible hope, one prayer at a time. No second chance. If I wanted children, adoption might be the only way. But at that time, adoption didn't feel right. We accepted the outcome, but inside, we still believed in a miracle-working God.

It was an ordinary Sunday, just days after the sperm test. As Kim got ready for work, she turned on the gospel radio. On air was our pastor, Andrew Evans, preaching about faith and the promises of God. He spoke of Abraham and Sarah—old, barren, and yet chosen. Their story, ancient yet alive, felt suddenly personal.

Something in Kim's heart stirred. It felt like God was whispering, "This promise is for you." Her spirit lit up with hope.

At the restaurant, she could barely hold in her excitement. "God's going to give us a child," she said.

I blinked. "Darling... I just had another sperm test and I'm still infertile. Remember?" I laughed, half amused, half trying not to hope. Surely this was her longing speaking. A beautiful hope, but impossible.

Part 2: A Promise Carried and Cradled

Few weeks later, Kim's mother and relatives visited from Malaysia. She played tour guide by day and restaurant helper by night. Tiredness crept into her bones. Her relatives teased, "Are you sure you're not pregnant?"

Even after they left, Kim slept more than usual. Just in case, we saw a doctor. A simple urine test. Positive.

But how?

I explained everything to the doctor. He smiled gently and recommended a blood test to be certain. We waited—half doubtful, half desperate. When the call came, it felt like the world stood still.

"She's pregnant."

Kim was pregnant.

We wept. We laughed. We worshipped. "Thank You, Lord," we repeated over and over. This child—this life—was nothing short of a miracle.

The potency of God's word is undeniable! He is a faithful and reliable God, steadfast in fulfilling His promises. Through the pages of the Bible, He extended promises to us, even in the face of medical evidence affirming my infertility. God fearlessly pledged us descendants.

Even as I had recently been declared infertile, He boldly conveyed to Kim, through the pastor's message, that she would conceive and bring forth a child! In moments of despair and hopelessness, He fearlessly bestowed promises upon us.

If God exhibits such boldness on our behalf, what have we to fear? Romans 8:31 assures us, (NIV) "If God is for us, who can be against us?" If God opens a door for us, who dares to shut it? Who can impede the grace that God desires to bestow upon us? Our heartfelt thanks to God, for in Christ, every promise of God is "Yes," and in Him, we say "Amen," to the glory of God (2 Corinthians 1:20).

But joy walked hand in hand with fear. My medical history, the medications, the doubts—what if something was wrong with the baby?

At the ultrasound, we chose silence—not out of denial, but as a quiet act of faith. The sterile room hummed with soft electronic beeps, and the sonographer's gentle voice guided us through each image on the screen. We offered no explanation of the impossible odds. No mention of past diagnoses or crushed hopes. Just silent prayers echoing in our hearts.

As the wand glided over Kim's belly, I held my breath, my eyes fixed on the screen. The flicker of a tiny heartbeat appeared—steady, strong. The sonographer looked up with a reassuring smile. "Everything looks normal," she said. "And…it's a girl."

Time stood still. A girl.

I glanced at Kim, whose eyes brimmed with silent tears. My own throat tightened. The moment was drenched in awe, fragile and sacred. We had walked through the valley of despair to arrive at this glimpse of promise—a heartbeat that echoed heaven's "Yes." The technician smiled, "Everything looks normal. It's a girl."

A daughter.

We were overwhelmed. But doubt, like shadows at dusk, still crept in. So we prayed. We reminded ourselves: God doesn't give stones when we ask for bread. (Matthew 7:7–11)

We chose to trust, to believe that the God who formed this child in the womb knew her before we ever did. Jeremiah 1:5 (NIV) rang true: "Before I formed you in the womb, I knew you; before you were born, I set you apart…"

Our belief in God's profound love for this child surpasses our own affection, and we recognize that the formation of this child is a manifestation of God's divine will, sovereignty, and ultimate glory. Despite our constant reminders that God has bestowed this child upon us out of His boundless love and grace, and that He will watch over and protect this child, we acknowledge our human frailty. Doubts and worries often find a place in our hearts.

Hebrews 11:1 teaches us that faith is the confidence in what we hope for and the assurance about what we do not see. However, the frailty of our faith becomes apparent when faced with the uncertainties of our surroundings, often requiring tangible evidence to strengthen our belief and bring about a sense of reassurance.

One Sunday in church, a kind elderly woman Kim had never seen before slipped quietly into the seat beside her. The worship team began to play, and the sanctuary filled with the rising swell of voices. Kim tried to join in, but her mind kept circling back to the unease that still stirred deep within. She held fast to God's promise, yet doubt clung stubbornly, like a shadow at the edge of light.

Out of the corner of her eye, she noticed the woman glance at her with a gentle, knowing smile. Then, without warning, the woman leaned in and whispered, "God asked me to tell you not to worry. This child is very special. God will bless and protect her."

The words struck Kim like a beam of light cutting through the fog, piercing straight to her heart. She turned to the stranger, her eyes wide. How could she possibly know the secret prayers whispered in the stillness of night? Tears gathered as Kim nodded slowly, sensing she was standing on holy ground. When she softly confessed some of her fears, the woman's smile deepened. "God told me to tell you," she said simply.

Kim felt her breath catch, not from fear, but from wonder. That Sunday morning, God had not only answered her prayers—He had wrapped them in human flesh and kindness. The message wasn't just a reassurance; it was a divine echo of the promise we were clinging to. Her heart swelled with quiet awe, strengthened anew by the whispered confirmation that Heaven was indeed watching over our miracle.

That encounter, like a thread of gold woven into cloth, anchored our hearts. God had heard us. He had seen us. And He had sent a messenger to say: "It is well."

This chapter, this whispered promise, taught us to hold fast to the word, not the world. God's faithfulness had not wavered. His word, soft as a whisper, had cradled us in the waiting.

And now, a heartbeat echoed within Kim. A song of grace. A promise alive.

Chapter 39

The Promise That Breathed

As Kim progressed into the fifth month of her pregnancy, an unexpected challenge arose—her father was diagnosed with lung cancer. Responding swiftly, she travelled to be by his side, quietly witnessing the harsh realities of chemotherapy—the sterile scent of hospital corridors, the dull beeping of machines, the gaunt look in her father's eyes. These moments carved a quiet grief into her heart. Yet even in sorrow, she carried the tender hope growing within her. With his condition stable, she returned after two weeks, determined to spend Christmas with me, wrapping her arms around two worlds—one fading, one just beginning.

Though Kim diligently fulfilled her duties at the restaurant, there remained a longing in her soul—to return to her professional field. When Mark, a friend from the newly established Eynesbury College, shared news of a part-time assistant accountant position, her eyes lit up. It wasn't the hours or the pay—it was the sense of identity, of purpose, that rekindled her spirit. To feel her mind reawaken, her skills engaged again, even for a few hours a week—it was a gift.

As the due date drew near, joy and anxiety danced in tandem. Despite God's promises, "what if" scenarios tugged at our peace. At night, we lay in bed whispering prayers through the quiet. Could we bear the weight of something going wrong? Were we ready—not just for birth, but for all that came after? Still, we chose trust. We clung to God's word like a lifeline in the dark.

Then, one ordinary night, the restaurant was bustling. Orders rang from the kitchen, chopsticks clinked against porcelain, and laughter echoed through the dining room. In the chaos, we called Kim to come help. She had been home, resting from college work, but answered our call without complaint. After the final table was cleared, we went home. The warm spray of the shower melted the tension from our bodies, and we collapsed onto the couch in quiet gratitude.

Then, a faint "pop."

Kim froze.

"I think… my water just broke."

The world tilted. My heart pounded. The moment we'd waited for had come.

We called the hospital. The nurse's voice was calm, reassuring. "Come in right away."

Driving through the night, Adelaide's streets were hushed under starlight. At the hospital, fluorescent lights greeted us, and the sharp antiseptic air pricked our senses awake. The doctor examined Kim and confirmed it—this was it.

The delivery room was bright but dimmed for calm. Monitors beeped. Nurses moved like whispers. Kim lay on the bed, weary but resolute. Hours passed. She tried to push, but her body trembled from exhaustion. She clenched my hand, sweat beading her brow. Still, she refused the epidural, determined to give birth in full strength. Her courage astounded me.

Eventually, her body pleaded for mercy. She requested the epidural. Relief came swiftly, washing over her like a breath of wind across still water. Her shoulders relaxed, her eyes closed briefly—an oasis in the storm.

But then, tension returned. The baby's heart rate dipped slightly. The monitor chirped with a new urgency. The doctor moved quickly. "We'll need the forceps."

Everything inside me tightened.

When our daughter finally emerged, the room filled with her piercing cry—a sound so raw, so beautiful, it sliced through the silence like a trumpet of grace.

Tears burst from my eyes. Not polite sobs—but deep, grateful weeping. I was trembling, undone. I had just witnessed a miracle.

The baby was placed in Kim's arms. Slimy, slippery, and tinged in a deep purplish hue—not the cherubic image we'd imagined. But to us, she was perfect. Kim clutched her close, her tears mingling with mine. Her fingers trembled as they brushed the baby's cheek. "She's here," she whispered. "She's really here."

I looked at Kim and saw the depth of her love etched across her tired face—astonishment, relief, and awe all woven together. We had walked through the valley of shadows. And here, in her arms, was the dawn.

The doctor's examination was thorough. Mother and daughter—healthy. Whole. Normal.

But nothing about this was normal.

This was divine.

The baby's cry echoed in our hearts long after the room quieted. Her tiny hands curled into fists. Her breaths, soft and rhythmic, were sacred songs. Kim and I sat in silence, drinking in the moment. I had imagined love before, but nothing had prepared me for this—this overwhelming tide that swelled in my chest, sweeping away every trace of fear.

We had doubted. We had feared. But God had come through—faithful as ever.

Even now, as I recall that night, I feel the warmth of Kim's hand in mine, the weight of our child nestled on her chest, and the unmistakable presence of God filling the room.

When Heaven touched Earth, it did not arrive with thunder or lightning. It came in a cry, in sweat and tears, in whispered prayers and trembling hands. It came in love—a love beyond reason, beyond science, beyond ourselves.

It came, and we were never the same.

This child was more than a daughter. She was a testimony.

PART 5

The Ending I Never Expected

"This vision is for a future time. It describes the end, and it will be fulfilled. If it seems slow in coming, wait patiently, for it will surely take place. It will not be delayed." Habakkuk 2:3 (NLT)

Chapter 40

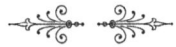

The Unfailing Love of the Father

The birth of our daughter marked more than a moment—it was a doorway into a sacred, unfamiliar dimension of love. I had always known my parents loved me, but only when I became a father did I truly understand the depth of that love. Parenthood didn't just introduce a new chapter in our lives; it opened a wellspring of selflessness, sacrifice, and devotion I had never known existed.

In the quiet hours of night, cradling our newborn, I found myself overwhelmed—not by exhaustion, though it was ever-present—but by awe. The tiniest coos, the scent of her delicate skin, the warmth of her body nestled against mine—each detail etched itself into my soul. The sleepless nights, the feedings, the diapers—these weren't burdens. They were sacred acts of love. Every sigh, every flutter of her eyelids, every trembling stretch of her fingers carried the weight of heaven.

Through the new lens of fatherhood, I began to understand why God calls us His children. That title isn't just symbolic—it's a window into His heart. Only through that sacred bond can we begin to grasp the kind of love He has for us.

As I held my daughter in my arms, something shifted. I loved her instinctively, unconditionally. I wanted to protect her, provide for her, and cherish her no matter what. That deep, natural affection opened my eyes to a truth I had long known in my head but was now beginning to feel in my soul: this is the lens through which God wants us to understand His love.

Just as I would do anything for my child, God's love surpasses even this noblest of human affections. Where our love may falter—growing tired, conditional, or wounded—His remains steady and unshakable. The love of a parent, I realized, is perhaps the clearest reflection of divine love we can experience on this side of eternity. It is fierce, patient, and forgiving. It's God's way of helping us experience, in human terms, the depth, tenderness, and persistence of His divine love. It's the kind of love God uses to help us understand His own.

1 John 4:8 (NIV) says, "God is love." Not just that He loves—but that love is who He is. And if I, with all my flaws, weaknesses, and failures, could love my daughter so completely, how much more could a perfect Father love us?

I began to believe—with absolute certainty—that nothing could ever diminish my love for her. Even if she were to rebel, stumble, or fail, my love would remain. That realization gave me more than just confidence as a father; it expanded my understanding of God's unrelenting grace.

Romans 8:38–39 (NIV) came alive in my heart like never before:

> "For I am convinced that neither death nor life, neither angels nor demons, neither the present nor the future, nor any powers… will be able to separate us from the love of God that is in Christ Jesus our Lord."

How do we begin to understand God's unconditional love? We don't fully—not until we see it through the eyes of a parent. He calls us His children so we might begin to understand what it means to be loved like that. The parent-child bond isn't just a helpful analogy—it's the very relationship God chose to describe the way He feels about us. And for me, that truth came alive the moment I became a father.

After much prayer and reflection, we named our baby girl 施恩—Shi En—which means "Bestowed (Shi) Grace (En)." It felt right, like heaven whispering confirmation. Her very existence was grace incarnate. We chose the English name Annabelle: "Anna" meaning grace and favor, "Belle" meaning beautiful. She was both.

Annabelle Shi En.

Even now, just saying her name stirs something in my chest.

Since the arrival of Shi En, Kim and my life has undergone significant changes. It's no longer just the two of us; we've had to adjust our habits and priorities, with a newfound focus on her. Being first-time parents, the excitement is immense, but it comes with its challenges. The initial three months were particularly demanding, and our lives were turned upside down. If we were in Malaysia, we could have sought the assistance of our parents or hired a confinement nanny. However, in Australia, navigating parenthood required us to manage everything independently. Unfortunately, the lack of proper postpartum care for Kim was a notable challenge we faced.

Originally, we had planned for my mom to join us and provide much-needed support during the postpartum period. Regrettably, her own health issues prevented her from making the trip. Kim's mom, burdened with the responsibility of caring for her ailing father, was also unable to come over. With my commitments at the restaurant, Kim found herself navigating the challenges of early motherhood largely on her own.

Those first three months were the hardest. Annabelle cried endlessly, inconsolably at times. Feed, burp, rock, repeat—but nothing soothed her for long. Doctors offered no clear answers. The constant crying, coupled with sleep deprivation, wore Kim down. Postpartum depression crept in quietly, shadowing even the bright moments.

There were days I came home to find Kim in tears, cradling a baby who wouldn't sleep. She questioned herself constantly—"Am I doing this right?" "Why won't she stop crying?" I tried to reassure her, to hold her and remind her she was enough. But no words could reach the deep place of weariness she had entered.

In the midst of it all, our daughter's presence—her smell of warm milk, her tiny fingers curling around ours, the rhythmic rise and fall of her chest as she slept—became our refuge and reminder of grace.

Chapter 41

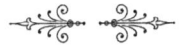

A Father's Final Prayer

Part I: The Urgency of Farewell

Prayer for Salvation in Crisis: As Annabelle turned three months old, we received distressing news from home—Kim's father's health had significantly deteriorated. Kim swiftly made the decision to take Annabelle back to visit her father, sensing that this visit might be their last.

After bidding farewell to Kim and Annabelle at the airport, I returned home and immediately began earnestly praying for the salvation of my father-in-law. Despite the fact that Kim's parents were devout Taoists with various idols at home, the prospect of them embracing God's salvation and converting to Christianity wasn't viewed with enthusiasm. Nonetheless, I held onto the hope that, even in these critical moments, my father-in-law could receive God's salvation. I believed that God was still reaching out to him, presenting an opportunity for a profound spiritual encounter.

A Divine Assurance from John 11: Following my prayer, I sought confirmation from God regarding the salvation of my father-in-law. I flipped open the Bible randomly on the table, my eyes landed on John 11:25, (NIV) where Jesus declares:

> "Jesus said to her, 'I am the resurrection and the life. The one who believes in me will live, even though they die; and whoever lives by believing in me will never die. Do you believe this?'" (John 11:25–26)

This verse narrates the account of Lazarus' death and the words spoken by Jesus to Mary and her sister Martha. Upon reading it, I sensed that God not only intended to offer salvation to my father-in-law but also aimed to bring healing. However, my doubts persisted, considering his limited exposure to Christianity. Besides attending his daughter's wedding in a church, he had never set foot in a church or interacted with Christians. Thus, I wondered, where would he experience God's healing and salvation?

Wrestling with Doubt and Choosing Faith: Still in doubt but I persisted in reading this chapter, verse 28–40:

> "When Martha heard this, she went back and called her sister Mary aside. 'The Teacher is here,' she said, 'and is asking for you.' When Mary heard this, she got up quickly and went to him. Now Jesus had not yet entered the village, but was still at the place where Martha had met him. When the Jews who had been with Mary in the house, comforting her, noticed how quickly she got up and went out, they followed her, supposing she was going to the tomb to mourn there. When Mary reached the place where Jesus was and saw him, she fell at his feet and said, 'Lord, if you had been here, my brother would not have died.' When Jesus saw her weeping, and the Jews who had

come along with her also weeping, he was deeply moved in spirit and troubled. 'Where have you laid him?' he asked. 'Come and see, Lord,' they replied. Jesus wept. Then the Jews said, 'See how he loved him!' But some of them said, 'Could not he who opened the eyes of the blind man have kept this man from dying?' Jesus, once more deeply moved, came to the tomb. It was a cave with a stone laid across the entrance. 'Take away the stone,' he said. 'But, Lord,' said Martha, the sister of the dead man, 'by this time there is a bad odor, for he has been there four days.' Then Jesus said, 'Did I not tell you that if you believe, you will see the glory of God?'"

When I reached verse 40, I felt that God was 'rebuking' my lack of faith. The verse says, "Did I not tell you that if you believed, you would see the glory of God?" Why do I always doubt God's words? His words are meant to be believed without hesitation!

A Final Moment and a Heavenly Reminder: Later in the evening, as soon as Kim returned home, I called her and shared the verses I had come across, emphasizing the assurance that her father would experience healing instead of succumbing to death. Kim, joined by her sisters, laid hands on him and fervently prayed. Regrettably, despite their efforts, he still passed away that very night. Thankfully, Kim managed to rush back in time to share a final moment with her father.

Part 2: Grace in the Final Hour

A Pastor's Timely Visit: Later on, Kim shared with me that a few days before her father's passing, a pastor from a church visited him and offered to pray for him. Remarkably, he willingly agreed to let the pastor pray for him! Though the specifics of what unfolded in that sacred moment of prayer elude our understanding, we remain open to God's revelation.

God's Word and the Assurance of Salvation: We thank the Lord that, in our most concern for and contemplation of his salvation, God, through the verses in John 11:25 - "I am the resurrection and the life. The one who believes in me will live, even though they die; and whoever lives by believing in me will never die. Do you believe this?" and verse 40 - "Did I not tell you that if you believed, you would see the glory of God?" has assured us that he is indeed in the arms of the Lord!

Is it mere coincidence that I randomly came across such relevant verses at that critical moment, or is it the hand of God at work? It's plausible that Kim's father, in a pivotal moment, made a life-altering decision to embrace Jesus as his Saviour when he willingly allowed the pastor to pray for him. The unfolding of God's salvation occurs when a person is willing to accept divine forgiveness, acknowledging Jesus as Lord. This simplicity epitomizes the natural essence of God's grace.

Romans 10 and the Simplicity of Faith: Romans 10:8–13 (NIV) states:

> "But what does it say? 'The word is near you; it is in your mouth and in your heart,' that is, the message concerning faith that we proclaim: If you declare with your mouth, 'Jesus is Lord,' and believe in your heart that God raised him from the dead, you will be saved. For it is with your heart that you believe and are justified, and it is with your mouth that you profess your faith and are saved. As Scripture says, 'Anyone who believes in him will never be put to shame.' For there is no difference between Jew and Gentile—the same Lord is Lord of all and richly blesses all

who call on him, for, 'Everyone who calls on the name of the Lord will be saved.'"

Not by Works, but by Grace: To attain God's salvation, it is essential not only to acknowledge our faults before God but also to accept Jesus as our Saviour. Ephesians 2:8 emphasizes that salvation comes through grace and faith, a gift from God and not something earned through our actions. It further clarifies that we are God's creation, designed in Christ Jesus for good works that God prepared beforehand.

It is crucial to understand that performing good deeds cannot be a barter for or an earning of God's salvation. If that were the case, it would not be a manifestation of God's grace, and we would have grounds for boasting. Salvation, as outlined in these verses, is a gift freely given by God and received through faith in Jesus Christ.

The Criminal at the Cross: A Case for Last-Minute Grace: When Jesus was crucified, there were two other criminals nailed to crosses alongside Him. Luke 23:39–43 (NIV):

> "One of the criminals who hung there hurled insults at him: 'Aren't you the Messiah? Save yourself and us!' But the other criminal rebuked him. 'Don't you fear God,' he said, 'since you are under the same sentence? We are punished justly, for we are getting what our deeds deserve. But this man has done nothing wrong.' Then he said, 'Jesus, remember me when you come into your kingdom.' Jesus answered him, 'Truly I tell you, today you will be with me in paradise.'"

It is crucial to note that Jesus explicitly declared, "Today you will be with me in paradise." This statement underscores the immediacy of receiving eternal life, with no delay until tomorrow, the day after, or after performing a certain number of good deeds.

Eternal life is granted instantaneously upon the expression of sincere faith and acknowledgment of Jesus, completely independent of any timeline or the need for accumulating good works. This powerful message reaffirms the simplicity and immediacy of God's gift of eternal salvation through faith in Jesus Christ.

The Transforming Power of Repentance: The Gospel of Mark tells us:

> "Those crucified with him also heaped insults on him."
> (Mark 15:32 NIV)

Both criminals crucified with Jesus initially mocked and insulted Him. However, one of the criminals later rebuked his counterpart, underwent a change of heart, apologized to Jesus, and received acceptance from Him. This nuanced portrayal in Mark adds depth to the narrative, highlighting the transformative journey of at least one of the criminals during the crucifixion event.

Praise be to the Lord for the profound and all-encompassing nature of God's mercy and grace! The incident involving the mocking criminal serves as a powerful illustration of how, despite having insulted and ridiculed Jesus just moments earlier, acceptance from Jesus swiftly followed as soon as he repented and sought forgiveness. This serves as a living testament to the truth articulated in Romans 10:9–10:

> "If you declare with your mouth, 'Jesus is Lord,' and believe in your heart that God raised him from the dead, you will be saved. For it is with your heart that you believe and are justified, and it is with your mouth that you profess your faith and are saved."

Additionally, it underscores the fundamental principle that salvation is not achieved through deeds or acts of goodness, as Ephesians 2:8–9 (NIV) declares:

> "For it is by grace you have been saved, through faith—and this is not from yourselves, it is the gift of God—not by works, so that no one can boast."

A Confident Hope in Salvation: I believe—despite all doubt, despite not witnessing it with my own eyes—that in his final days, Kim's father encountered the saving grace of God. Just as the thief on the cross did. Just as I had.

And so I rest in that hope. That love, indeed, never fails.

Chapter 42

A New Season Begins

After running the restaurant business for a year and a half, the partnership between Peter and me began to fray. The cracks, subtle at first, deepened with time—likely rooted in an imbalance of effort and capability. I humbly acknowledge that I lacked proper training, and in Peter's eyes, my role may have seemed peripheral, dispensable. His capacity to juggle tasks—seemingly doing the work of three—only magnified my own modest abilities.

Eventually, Peter came to me with a difficult proposal: to dissolve our partnership. It was a weighty decision, one that would affect not just my livelihood but Kim's as well. Her part-time job offered only a few hours a week, and the restaurant had been our primary source of income. Despite Kim's apprehensions, a quiet peace settled in my heart. I agreed to relinquish my shares.

With the restaurant chapter closing, a long-held dream stirred once more in my spirit—to study theology. I had always imagined enrolling in Bible College after spending more time in the business world, believing that season would come later. But God, in His perfect timing, opened the door far sooner than I expected. In hindsight, I realize that had I continued in the restaurant, I might never have paused long enough to follow that calling.

This turning point became an invitation to step into a new season. I enrolled at our church's theological college almost immediately. Peter kindly offered me a full-time role at the restaurant, but I chose to work only two evenings a week. Though it drastically reduced our income, it gave us something more valuable—time. Time for our family, time for friendships, time for church. That shift brought a joy money could never buy.

Meanwhile, Kim's workplace was growing, and so were her hours. But her schedule remained beautifully flexible. She often began her work after I finished college for the day. When needed, a dear friend graciously helped us look after Annabelle. In every way, God provided. Just as Psalm 23 (KJV) declares, *"The Lord is my shepherd; I shall not want."*

To supplement our modest income, we welcomed a boarding student from Indonesia into our home. Despite her wealthy background, she carried herself with humility, warmth, and respect. There was no trace of entitlement—only gratitude. Her parents, appreciative of our care, occasionally sent us gifts.

Hosting her turned out to be not just a blessing, but a joy. It eased our financial burden and gave her a second home. Encouraged by the experience and blessed with the space—our house had four bedrooms—we opened our doors to another student. This ministry of hospitality grew into a rhythm of grace. It wasn't just shelter we were offering, but a sense of belonging. The smiles of our boarders and the thankfulness of their parents became gentle reminders of God's provision through community.

Looking back, I marvel at how God rearranged the pieces of our lives with such deliberate tenderness. A closed door in business opened a path to purpose. A financial stretch drew us closer in faith. Hosting students became not just a necessity, but a ministry.

And in every detail, we witnessed the quiet faithfulness of our Shepherd—leading us beside still waters, restoring our souls, and guiding us into green pastures.

Chapter 43

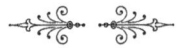

A Second Heartbeat

*"Children are a heritage from the Lord, offspring a reward from him.
Like arrows in the hands of a warrior are children born in one's youth.
Blessed is the man whose quiver is full of them. They will not be put to shame
when they contend with their opponents in court"*
—Psalm 127:3–4 (NIV)

Despite the immeasurable joy Annabelle brought into our lives, Kim and I chose not to hastily expand our family. Though I had once told Kim I wanted at least four children, we didn't feel the urgency to grow our family immediately. We approached our planning with prayer and careful thought, content with the grace already entrusted to us.

But God had a different plan. When Annabelle was a year and a half old, Kim unexpectedly became pregnant again. It wasn't what we had anticipated, but our hearts swelled with joy—*"Children are a heritage from the Lord."* Yet that joy was brief. Within the first trimester, we experienced a miscarriage. Though grief swept over us, we clung to the belief that God's purposes were not thwarted.

Not long after, God stirred hope again. Kim conceived once more. This time, however, caution tempered our joy. Many reminded us of the risks: the closeness of pregnancies, the physical toll, the emotional vulnerability after loss. We proceeded gently, placing each step into God's hands, though fear often crept into our thoughts.

And in those moments, we forgot Hebrews 11:6 (NIV)— *"And without faith it is impossible to please God, because anyone who comes to him must believe that he exists and that he rewards those who earnestly seek him."* We truly deserved a rebuke for our doubts. This child was not born of our planning but of God's. If it was His gift, why should we fear? Our human tendency is to take control, to worry first and pray later. But the truth is—we must surrender first and trust always.

I also wrestled with an unusual fear: Would I love this child as deeply as I loved Annabelle? Would my affection feel divided, or worse, unequal? Annabelle and I had built such a strong bond. I was afraid that the love wouldn't come as naturally with the new baby.

Throughout Kim's pregnancy, we were convinced we were expecting a boy. We had already chosen his name—Joshua, a name rich in biblical courage and promise. His Chinese name, 启恩, Qi En, meant "Revelation of Grace." From the womb, he was embraced with prayer and dreams.

When Joshua was born—healthy and full-term—I had the incredible blessing of witnessing his arrival. And in that instant, every fear I had about not being able to love him enough melted away. The love I felt was just as deep and complete as what I had felt for Annabelle. My heart didn't divide—it expanded. Each child was a unique gift, an irreplaceable joy. Joshua's presence didn't lessen Annabelle's; it multiplied the joy in our home.

That moment revealed a spiritual truth: God's love is never divided. It's full, constant, and never diminished by being shared. Yet we often imagine God loves others more—those who are more faithful, more obedient, more deserving. But that's a human distortion.

As John 3:16 (NIV) declares, "For God so loved the world that he gave his one and only Son, that whoever believes in him shall not perish but have eternal life." His love is not performance-based. He doesn't love a pastor more than a prodigal. His love is unwavering. You can't earn it—and you can't lose it. "For God does not show favoritism." (Romans 2:11, NIV)

Looking back, I'm struck by how often we underestimate the vastness of God's love. As a father, I didn't have to divide my affection between my children—it multiplied. And if my flawed human heart could love like that, how much more must the perfect Father love each of us—personally and completely.

In a world where love often feels conditional, this truth is both humbling and liberating: God's love is not something to achieve—it is a gift to receive. And understanding that didn't just deepen my love as a parent—it filled me with awe for the Father who first loved us.

This time, my parents were able to visit us during Joshua's birth. Their presence was not just helpful—it was healing. For Kim, it was a balm to her body and spirit. She was no longer alone in the quiet, uncertain moments of early motherhood. This time, her days were filled with the gentle clinking of kitchen pots, the aroma of ginger wine chicken soup simmering on the stove, and the comforting presence of my mother's hands—strong, experienced, and full of care.

Each day, my mother prepared nourishing meals, her way of pouring love into Kim's recovery. My father, though quieter, carried Joshua with tender pride, whispering little blessings into his grandson's ears. Their support transformed our home. Laughter returned to the corners that once echoed with exhaustion. Evenings became moments of shared joy—Kim resting in warmth, my parents doting over their grandson, and me standing quietly at the edge of it all, soaking in the gift of family.

Compared to Annabelle's birth, when Kim bore the burden of postpartum recovery largely on her own, this was a season of restoration. It was as if God had heard the silent prayers we didn't know how to pray during our first journey into parenthood—and answered them this time with grace in flesh and comfort in presence.

With a baby boy now in our arms, our home pulsed with deeper joy. A second heartbeat echoed in our lives—not just from a new child, but from the rhythm of God's grace, once again revealing His faithfulness through life, love, and legacy.

Chapter 44

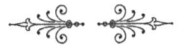

A House of Blessings

Two and a half years at the theological college passed swiftly, and I finally fulfilled my long-held desire to complete the program. Beyond the accumulation of biblical knowledge, the most crucial takeaway from college was the cultivation of a deeper, more intimate relationship with God. While many of my classmates eagerly stepped into ministry roles after graduation, I found myself burdened for the Chinese community but without a clear sense of direction.

As I pondered the path ahead, an unexpected door opened. The house next door to ours went up for auction. The government valuation was a modest $120,000. The auction attracted little attention, and though the bidding reached $140,000, the owner refused to sell. Later, we decided to make an offer—a bold and unusual one: $99,999.99. To our astonishment, they accepted it without negotiation!

We were ecstatic. It was an unheard-of price, significantly below the government's valuation and well beneath typical market expectations. Most properties in our area were listed at twenty to fifty percent above their government assessments then. To secure this home at such a favourable price was undeniably a miracle. We could only attribute it to God's favour and blessing.

This home became part of a larger vision we had been nurturing—to grow our boarding student ministry. With thoughtful renovations, we transformed the house into a five-bedroom residence tailored to welcome students from overseas. The timing was impeccable. I had just completed my studies, and my parents were visiting to help with the upcoming arrival of Joshua. Their assistance during the renovation period was indispensable.

This boarding venture turned out to be a timely provision. With Kim working outside the home, I could manage part-time work while being present with our two beloved children. It allowed me the rare privilege of being deeply involved in their early development—a privilege I cherished more than any professional pursuit.

Approximately five and a half years after Joshua's birth, our home was once again filled with joyous anticipation. God blessed us with another child—a daughter, whom we named Faith.

The arrival of Faith added yet another thread of wonder and warmth to the fabric of our family. We selected her name intentionally. In English, Faith speaks to trust, belief, and reliance on God's promises. Her Chinese name, 慧恩, Hui En, wisdom and grace, reflects our hope that she would walk in wisdom and embody the grace she was given.

As she grew, Faith brought with her a sense of completeness. Her presence affirmed the richness of God's gifts and deepened the joy in our family. She was not a replacement or repetition but a unique expression of God's creativity and love.

Parenting Annabelle, Joshua, and Faith has stretched our hearts in ways we never imagined. Each child is a testament to God's faithfulness, a reminder that His blessings are perfectly timed and abundantly good. The journey has been filled with laughter, tears, prayers, and miracles. Through every chapter, God has proven that His plans are higher, His timing perfect, and His love unending.

Truly, our home had become what we never anticipated but always needed: a house of blessings.

To pledge our allegiance and express our heartfelt gratitude to this beautiful country, Kim and I became Australian citizens on the 23rd of April, 2003. It was more than a change of legal status—it was a heartfelt declaration of belonging. This land had become our home in every sense of the word. It had welcomed us, sheltered us, healed us, and blessed us beyond what we ever imagined. Here, we had found community, purpose, and the freedom to grow our family and faith.

Standing together during the citizenship ceremony, with hands on our hearts and eyes filled with emotion, we felt the weight and wonder of the moment. We weren't just pledging allegiance to a flag—we were acknowledging all the unseen graces that had led us to that point. Australia had given us so much: safety, opportunity, friendship, and above all, a new life rooted in hope.

It was also a deeply spiritual moment. For us, it wasn't merely the fulfillment of an immigration process; it was part of God's unfolding plan. We sensed that this nation was not only a place of refuge, but also a field of assignment—a land where we were called to serve, love, and make a difference.

Then came the singing of our new national anthem. As the words *"Australians all let us rejoice, for we are young and free"* rang through the room, I was overwhelmed. Tears welled in my eyes—not just for the journey behind us, but for the promise ahead. In that song, I heard not only national pride but God's kindness echoing through every line. Becoming citizens felt like more than a civic step; it was a sacred milestone in a much bigger story: God's story of restoration, promise, and purpose.

We called Australia home that day. And we *still call Australia Home.*

Chapter 45

Bridges of Belonging

The family group in our church experienced a season of vibrant growth and divine momentum. To better serve its expanding members, the leadership discerned the need to divide the group into two distinct paths: one tailored for students, and the other for families. Since the heart of our group leader leaned toward student ministry, they approached Kim and me about stepping into the role of leading the newly formed family group. Despite my theological training, I initially resisted the idea. I hadn't envisioned myself in leadership and provided a litany of reasons why I wasn't ready. Yet the leader's persistence, care, and confidence in us gradually softened our hesitation.

After prayerful deliberation, we accepted the challenge—not because we felt perfectly equipped, but because we saw a need and believed God would supply what we lacked. Our fellowship gathered in Mandarin. I focused on preparing the teaching and discussion content, while Kim gracefully led worship on the keyboard.

To our surprise, the first gathering wasn't as daunting as we feared. The warmth, enthusiasm, and mutual support of those present ignited a sense of gratitude and fulfilment in our hearts. We began with a small, close-knit circle—just over ten adults, a few with children in tow.

As word spread, newly arrived Chinese immigrants began to join us. Many had yet to encounter the Gospel, but they were drawn by the joy and authenticity of our fellowship. At times, our living room brimmed with thirty or more attendees. Yet we recognized a limitation—their limited English proficiency made participating in our broader church services challenging. To address this, we lovingly directed them to a Chinese-speaking church in the city where they could grow in faith more comfortably.

Watching these newcomers flourish in their new spiritual home brought us immense joy. We witnessed firsthand the power of community to transform isolation into belonging, and uncertainty into rootedness. It reminded us that the Church is not bound by walls or languages—it is bound by love.

As our group continued to grow and more English-speaking families joined, we prayerfully transitioned from Mandarin to English, widening our circle of inclusivity. God, in His gracious timing, brought Andrew and Linda to serve alongside us. Their presence was a profound blessing. Andrew's quiet strength and Linda's anointed gift in leading worship elevated our gatherings into moments of divine connection.

With growth came the need for more space. We moved our meetings to the church premises, a transition that mirrored our broader vision—building not just a gathering, but a community. More than ten families and twenty children now joined us fortnightly. To serve the diverse needs of our little ones, we introduced junior and senior groups, ensuring each child received guidance appropriate to their stage of life and faith.

These intentional efforts weren't merely administrative—they were deeply spiritual. We believed every soul, every child, every family deserved to feel seen, known, and loved. Our mission wasn't to grow numbers—it was to build a spiritual family anchored in God's Word and sustained by His grace.

The Asian community within our church also began to swell. While several small groups existed, a deeper sense of unity was lacking. We heard the silent cry of many who longed for deeper connection, especially among those who didn't feel at home in an English-speaking context.

With our pastor's full blessing, we launched the 'Asian Connect' Group. This was more than a program—it was a movement. A place where Asians from different backgrounds could find spiritual kinship, cultural resonance, and Gospel-centred fellowship. It became a bridge—not only for believers but also for non-Christians seeking something more.

Our fortnightly gatherings quickly grew to over 150 people. We marvelled at the hunger—for connection, for truth, for hope. These gatherings breathed life into our church, offering sanctuary and strength to many. Recognizing the growing needs of the Asian community, the church appointed a wonderful couple from Malaysia to lead the ministry: Pastor Michael a Malaysian Indian, and his Malaysian Chinese wife, Chiew Har.

We believed then—and still believe—that no one should walk alone. That community is not optional in faith, but essential. And through Asian Connect, we glimpsed the heart of the early church: diverse, united, and radically generous with love.

After several fruitful years, Asian Connect was brought to a close. There was no scandal, no conflict—just a shift in vision. The church leadership, sensing the need to build unity across cultures rather than along them, decided to move away from culturally specific ministries. Without a dedicated pastor to shepherd it forward, we let it go with grateful hearts. Still, for many, the farewell left an ache.

But as one chapter closed, another quietly opened. A fresh need arose—Mandarin-speaking parents and friends longed for fellowship in their heart language. Together with Andrew and Linda, we began a Mandarin fellowship. It was modest at first, but quickly grew.

We also introduced live Mandarin translation during Sunday services to support those with limited English. It wasn't perfect—we didn't have a professional translator—but we made it work. Over time, the Mandarin fellowship blossomed into a full-fledged Mandarin church, led by Pastor Michael and Chiew Har. Their marriage beautifully reflected God's heart for cross-cultural unity—a Malaysian Indian pastor and his Malaysian Chinese wife, both non-Mandarin speaking, leading a Mandarin-speaking congregation. Together, they embodied the very diversity and harmony our church had come to represent.

This church met weekly in a hotel following the English service, at a time when our city campus was still seeking a permanent home. The effort required to set up and pack down each Sunday was enormous, and the church leadership eventually re-evaluated its direction.

They considered hiring a Mandarin pastor but ultimately decided against it. The reasons were practical—modest growth, resource limitations—and philosophical—a desire to unify the church body across cultures rather than segment it. Thus, the Mandarin church concluded its final service after two years.

Looking back, we see the fingerprints of God in every chapter. In every transition, every gathering, every farewell, His grace remained. We learned that ministry is not measured by longevity but by love. And in loving well, we fulfilled His call.

From living room gatherings to church halls, from Mandarin prayers to English praise, from breaking bread to building bridges, we have tasted the beauty of community in its purest form: ordinary people drawn together by an extraordinary God.

Chapter 46

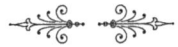

Ambassadors of Reconciliation

Part I: A Lettered Witness

Having embraced faith in the Lord, a natural inclination arose within me to share the boundless grace and love that I found in Him, particularly with those closest to me—my family. The joy that flows from encountering the transformative power of Christ compels the heart to share. It is as if the soul, set free by grace, cannot help but cry out for others to taste and see that the Lord is good.

2 Corinthians 5:17-21 (NIV) declares:

> "Therefore, if anyone is in Christ, the new creation has come: The old has gone, the new is here! All this is from God, who reconciled us to himself through Christ and gave us the ministry of reconciliation: that God was reconciling the world to himself in Christ, not counting people's sins against them. And he has committed to us the message

of reconciliation. We are therefore Christ's ambassadors, as though God were making his appeal through us. We implore you on Christ's behalf: Be reconciled to God. God made him who had no sin to be sin for us, so that in him we might become the righteousness of God."

This passage spoke deeply to me. It reminded me that my faith was not only personal but purposeful. I had become a new creation, and with that transformation came a calling: to become Christ's ambassador and messenger of reconciliation.

Back in the 1980s and 90s, reaching out to family overseas was not simple. The internet, email, or instant communication tools did not exist. Phone calls from Australia to Malaysia were prohibitively expensive, costing AUD $1.50 per minute. Letters became the most feasible and heartfelt way to communicate.

So I wrote.

I wrote long, reflective letters, sharing the gospel and what Christ had done in my life. Since my single life then held few personal updates, I focused instead on the beauty of the gospel. Where conversations might invite interruptions or disinterest, letters offered space—time to ponder, reread, and reflect. Though they seldom replied about matters of faith, I held to the truth that God's Word would not return void. I believed that as long as I sowed, God could water and bring growth.

Acts 16:31 (NIV) kept my hope alive: "Believe in the Lord Jesus, and you will be saved—you and your household."

Still, discouragement would creep in. I often wondered: Had I pushed too hard? Was I overbearing? I understood that salvation is not something I could orchestrate. Only God can turn hearts. My role was to love, testify, and trust.

One particular incident stands out. I used an analogy while talking with my parents, describing how it grieves God when we reject His love—like a parent being rejected by their child. Tragically, they misunderstood. My mother believed I was truly turning my back on them. Influenced by a concerned cousin who warned that Christians often abandon their families, my parents were devastated. My mother cried for days and refused to speak to me. I felt helpless, heartbroken, and guilt-ridden.

In response, I poured my heart into another letter—explaining that my faith did not negate my love for them. On the contrary, it deepened it.

I explained that honouring our parents isn't just a traditional value passed down in Asian culture—it's actually a command from God. In the Ten Commandments, after the first few that speak about our relationship with God, the very next one is this: "Honour your father and mother." It's not a suggestion; it's a divine instruction. And it's the only commandment that comes with a promise—that if we do, we'll live a long and blessed life. That shows just how much God values family and respect across generations.

I shared Deuteronomy 21:18-21, illustrating the seriousness God placed on honouring parents, as well as Deuteronomy 27:16, which places a curse on those who dishonour them. From the New Testament, I cited Ephesians 6:1-2 (NIV):

> "Children, obey your parents in the Lord, for this is right. 'Honour your father and mother' —which is the first commandment with a promise— so that it may go well with you and that you may enjoy long life on the earth."

The Amplified Bible portrays parents as God's earthly representatives. Failing to honour them reflects poorly on how we honour our Heavenly Father. I wanted my parents to know that my love for them was not diminished by my faith—it was magnified.

Thankfully, they received my letter with grace. Our relationship was restored.

Part II: A Greater Presence

Years later, my parents began visiting us in Australia regularly. During their stays, I would take them to Chinese-speaking churches, hoping they would encounter the same faith that had transformed my life. On one occasion, a close friend gently shared the gospel with them and encouraged them to accept Christ. My mother seemed open and sincere; she listened attentively and nodded with quiet conviction. My father, on the other hand, remained more reserved—he listened silently, but I sensed he was still holding back.

After they returned to Malaysia, something changed. My mother stopped worshipping idols. It was a quiet, unspoken decision—but a deeply significant one. My father, however, didn't take the same step. The idols remained on the household altar, untouched. In many ways, that altar came to represent the line between openness and resistance, between softening hearts and lingering traditions.

Then came an unforgettable moment—one that shook them deeply.

My mother had fallen ill and, overwhelmed with fear, began to suspect that something "unclean" was tormenting her. One of her sisters, concerned, brought both my parents to a temple to consult a spirit medium. After performing his rituals, the medium declared that her spirit was fine. Still, he insisted on making a spiritual visit to their home.

But what happened next stunned everyone.

As soon as the spirit medium arrived outside the house, he paused. He scanned the space and announced that the idols inside were empty—there was no spiritual presence in them. Then, without warning, his face turned pale. Visibly shaken, he took a step back.

"I can't go in," he stammered. "There's a massive power in that house—something far greater than me."

Without another word, he left in a panic.

My parents were stunned.

I explained to them: that presence was none other than Jesus Christ—living, reigning, powerful. 1 John 4:4 (NIV) says:

> "You, dear children, are from God and have overcome them, because the one who is in you is greater than the one who is in the world."

I also quoted Philippians 2:6-11 (NIV):

> "Who, being in very nature God, did not consider equality with God something to be used to his own advantage; rather, he made himself nothing by taking the very nature of a servant... Therefore God exalted him to the highest place... that at the name of Jesus every knee should bow... and every tongue acknowledge that Jesus Christ is Lord."

I hoped this supernatural encounter would prompt my parents to fully embrace Christ. Though they had not yet made a decisive commitment, I continue to pray. I believe God used even that encounter to declare His sovereignty. And His love for my parents, like mine, remains unwavering.

We are not responsible for saving anyone—that is the work of the Holy Spirit. But we are ambassadors. We carry the message of reconciliation. And sometimes, we plant seeds. Other times, we witness miracles. Always, we trust in the one who makes all things grow.

Chapter 47

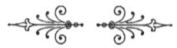

When Heaven Brushed the Ceiling – A Father's Night of Revelation

Part I: The Unseen Glory Unveiled

During my parents' visit in 2012, our modest home lacked a spare bedroom, and so, with quiet reverence, the living room was transformed into a resting place for them. It was there, beneath the unassuming ceiling of that humble space, that heaven chose to unveil its mysteries.

One evening, after finishing a Chinese TV series, my father turned off the lights and prepared for bed. As he lay in stillness, ready to surrender to sleep, something extraordinary caught his eye—a vision so delicate and radiant it could only be divine. Spanning the entire ceiling were flowers, delicate as silver threads, luminous and crystalline, glowing with a beauty no human tongue could capture. They shimmered like dew-kissed stars spun in moonlight.

Startled, he rubbed his eyes, suspecting a dream or a trick of light. But the vision remained. Moments stretched like eternity—for an unknown sacred minute seemed eternity—as heaven's embroidery adorned the ceiling. Then, as silently as it had appeared, it faded into the shadows.

Perplexed, he wondered if we had decorated the ceiling during the day—surely such marvel must have a human explanation. But nothing could explain the ethereal bloom.

Reflecting on the many home group gatherings we hosted in that room—filled with praise and worship—he began to wonder: Could this be the lingering glory of God? He waited two days before sharing the vision, unsure how it might be received.

When he finally spoke, he did so with earnestness and wonder. Though I considered the possibility of tired eyes or screen-induced illusions, his sincerity and delight were unmistakable. He asked if it might return, and my mother, in jest, said he must wake her if it did—she, too, longed to glimpse heaven's artistry.

Part II: Grapes of Glory

Astonishingly, that very evening, another vision arrived.

Again, after turning off the lights and lying down, he beheld a new miracle. This time, it wasn't flowers, but grapes—clusters of them, radiant as silver and crystal, suspended from the ceiling like celestial fruit from the vineyards of heaven. Awestruck, he woke my mother, yet once again, her eyes met only darkness.

The grapes glowed and shimmered before dissolving, just like the flowers before. My father, half-amused, half-humbled, joked that it should have been durian—his favourite fruit!

He was enraptured by these nightly revelations and began to long for them, as one thirsts for dreams that taste of eternity. Even young Hui En wanted to sleep with them in hopes of seeing such wonders.

We sensed a message hidden in the mystery. Was God unveiling something sacred to my father? I began to pray, seeking clarity.

Part III: Waters from the Throne

Two nights later, the heavens opened a third time.

After the usual routine, as my father settled beneath the same ordinary ceiling, it was transformed once again into something divine. This time, it resembled a vast expanse of crystalline water, luminous and alive. Within its depths, bubble-like orbs shimmered and rose, like spirits dancing upward in a living sea of glass. It reminded him of the undersea tunnel at a Singapore aquarium—but far more majestic. Joy and peace flooded his soul, yet part of him feared: what if the ceiling gave way?

He roused my mother again. Yet, as before, the vision belonged to him alone.

Why did these divine images come only to him? And why three nights in a row? The answer unfolded gradually, a sacred whisper in the soul: God was calling my father. These visions were not for entertainment or awe—they were an invitation to salvation.

Part IV: The Meaning Behind the Visions

After Dad shared the third vision with us—the lake of crystal-clear water—I felt something shift within me. It was as though God lifted the veil and gave me the interpretation. What once seemed mysterious suddenly made sense. These visions were not just dreams—they were divinely ordered, a spiritual roadmap. Each image built upon the last, gently leading my father, step by step, from belief to salvation, and finally, to the promise of eternal life.

The sequence of visions—flowers, grapes, and a crystal-like lake—held profound spiritual significance. Each was not random or decorative, but symbolic of a divine invitation. Together, they formed a spiritual progression: from initial belief, to salvation, and ultimately, to eternal life.

Each vision carried a message rooted in Scripture and spoke to a different stage of spiritual awakening:

- **The flowers represented belief.**
  Though glorious, the flowers were not fruit. They were beautiful but fleeting—like belief without commitment. Delicate and full of potential, they mirrored faith in its earliest form. As James 2:19 (ESV) warns, *"Even the demons believe—and shudder."* Belief alone is not enough, yet it is still the first step. It shows the heart is stirring, like a bud beginning to open.
- **The grapes symbolized salvation.**
  Grapes, among the most frequently mentioned fruits in Scripture, signify fruitfulness and God's desire for a bountiful life. But they don't appear overnight. They require time, care, and connection to the source. Jesus said, *"I am the vine; you are the branches. If you remain in me and I in you, you will bear much fruit"* (John 15:5 (NIV)). Grapes reflect abiding faith—belief that has matured into surrender, producing the fruit of a transformed life.
- **The crystal-like lake reflected eternal life.**
  Its stillness and purity spoke of peace beyond understanding. It reminded me of Revelation 4:6 (NIV), which describes *"a sea of glass, clear as crystal, before the throne,"* and Revelation 22:1: *"Then the angel showed me the river of the water of life, clear as crystal, flowing from the throne of God and of the Lamb."* This final vision

pointed beyond the present—toward the eternal promise of God, where suffering ends and the soul finds perfect rest.

Whenever I asked my dad if he believed in Jesus Christ, his answer was always yes. But when I gently pressed further—whether he had accepted Jesus as his Saviour—he would shrug it off with a casual, "It doesn't matter, maybe later. There's no rush. Once I accept, many things become restricted, and I can't enjoy my favourite vegetarian dishes at the temple."

But through the three visions God gave him, I sensed a divine urging—that the time to accept Jesus had come.

The flowers in his vision represented belief—the first step in acknowledging Jesus. But belief alone, without confession or surrender, is not enough. Scripture makes this clear: even acknowledging that Jesus died for our sins does not constitute a saving relationship with Him. God desires more than mere mental agreement. He wants a heart response that leads to action.

It's like someone offering you a gift—say, a car. You might believe they're sincere. But unless you reach out and accept it, the car will never truly be yours. Belief is essential, but it must be followed by a response.

My dad's belief was like a flower—beautiful, alive, and full of potential. But God desires more than a blossom; He desires fruit. That fruit is salvation: the eternal life promised in the river of the water of life, flowing from the throne of God. And to move from flower to fruit, my dad must take the next step: not just believing in his heart, but confessing with his mouth and declaring Jesus as Lord.

Only through that active response can he fully receive the salvation—the fruit— of eternal life and the living water God has already prepared for him. This is the heart of faith: belief that blossoms into action, and action that bears eternal fruit.

Chapter 48

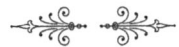

The Day of Decision

Part I: The Promise Fulfilled

Upon presenting this interpretation to my dad, he acknowledged its reasonability and found himself notably surprised. However, the critical next step of acceptance was yet to be taken. The visions had served as a powerful revelation, laying out a spiritual journey that invites him to deepen his relationship with God and embrace the promise of eternal life.

Two days later, on April 16th, Carmen, a recent graduate residing in our student accommodation, and her family visited us in Australia to celebrate her graduation. Carmen's father, Mr. Yu, had reached out to my father over the phone about three years ago when my mother was unwell in Malaysia. Initially, Mr. Yu had planned to visit and offer prayers for my mom, but due to various reasons, the visit never materialized, and they hadn't met in person in Malaysia.

Upon their arrival, Mr. Yu immediately extended an apology to my parents for not visiting earlier. In a light-hearted manner, he even remarked that the matter had kept him from having a restful night's sleep over the past three years. He continued by expressing that if they did not embrace Christianity that day, he wouldn't leave!

I encouraged my dad to share his recent profound vision experiences with Mr. Yu and explained the significance of these visions. Mr. Yu then cited certain scriptures and invited my parents to decide to accept Jesus as their Saviour. Agreeing with Mr. Yu's guidance, my parents prayed to accept the Lord Jesus during this visit. In the course of the prayer, Mr. Yu even shared a prophecy for my dad, foreseeing that he would lead many people to the Lord, drawing a parallel to Moses in the Bible.

All thanks and praise be to the Lord; every bit of glory belongs to Him. I am profoundly thankful to witness my dear parents finally making the decision to accept the Lord Jesus as their Saviour. It is a genuine honour for me and has lifted the heaviest burden for their salvation from my heart.

Despite my continuous prayers for my parents, there were moments when I doubted if they would ever embrace faith in the Lord. While they didn't express opposition to Christianity, their responses appeared highly improbable. I had encountered numerous testimonies of elderly parents and staunch sceptics experiencing a miraculous transformation in their faith journey, but the prospect seemed insurmountable for my parents. I entertained the thought that maybe God hadn't heard my prayers. However, once again, God demonstrated that I was mistaken; it was a testament to my own faltering faith.

Part II: The Silence and the Splendour

When God Delays: Zechariah

I recalled a story from the Gospel of Luke, Chapter 1:5–18 (NIV) "In the time of Herod king of Judea, there was a priest named Zechariah, who belonged to the priestly division of Abijah; his wife Elizabeth was also a descendant of Aaron. Both of them were righteous in the sight of God, observing all the Lord's commands and decrees blamelessly. But they were childless because Elizabeth was not able to conceive, and they were both very old. Once when Zechariah's division was on duty and he was serving as priest before God, he was chosen by lot, according to the custom of the priesthood, to go into the temple of the Lord and burn incense. And when the time for the burning of incense came, all the assembled worshipers were praying outside. Then an angel of the Lord appeared to him, standing at the right side of the altar of incense. When Zechariah saw him, he was startled and was gripped with fear. But the angel said to him: 'Do not be afraid, Zechariah; your prayer has been heard. Your wife Elizabeth will bear you a son, and you are to call him John (the Baptist). He will be a joy and delight to you, and many will rejoice because of his birth, for he will be great in the sight of the Lord. He is never to take wine or other fermented drink, and he will be filled with the Holy Spirit even before he is born. He will bring back many of the people of Israel to the Lord their God. And he will go on before the Lord, in the spirit and power of Elijah, to turn the hearts of the parents to their children and the disobedient to the wisdom of the righteous—to make ready a people prepared for the Lord.' Zechariah asked the angel, 'How can I be sure of this? I am an old man and my wife is well along in years.'"

When God finally chose to answer the prayers of the aging priest Zechariah, he and his wife were well past their childbearing years. It's conceivable that they had long abandoned the idea of having their own children, and the prospect seemed improbable. Zechariah's reaction to the angel's announcement about their old age suggests that he might have considered it a jest or a prank. The question arose: Why would God choose this time, when they were no longer in the prime of their youth?

It is unlikely that Zechariah's first prayer for a child coincided with his temple duties. Rather, it seems plausible that he and his wife Elizabeth had been fervently praying for a child for an extended period—perhaps even on the night of their wedding, beseeching God for the blessing of offspring. While contemporary couples may not immediately contemplate starting a family on their wedding night, in that historical context, procreation was often a primary purpose of marriage.

In their supplications to God, I imagine that on their wedding night, Zechariah and Elizabeth expressed, "Lord, grant us a child before our first wedding anniversary!" However, God did not promptly fulfil their request. Instead, He chose to respond when they were advanced in age. How peculiar and unexpected!

This delay in divine response does not imply that God was deaf to Zechariah's prayers, nor did He postpone listening until Zechariah was old. Rather, it underscores God's perfect timing, comprehensive plan, and unforeseeable arrangements.

Frequently, God initiates His work when it is least anticipated! If Zechariah and Elizabeth had been blessed with a child earlier, that child might have missed the profound mission of preparing the way for the Lord.

Years later, when John the Baptist commenced his ministry, urging people to repent as the kingdom of God is imminent, he faced questioning about his identity from Jewish leaders. In response, he turned to the prophecy from the book of Isaiah (Isaiah 40:3). As documented in the Gospel of John in the New Testament, John the Baptist declared, "I am the voice of one calling in the wilderness, 'Make straight the way for the Lord'" (John 1:23, NIV).

John explicitly stated that he was not the long-awaited Messiah, Elijah, or "the Prophet." Instead, he identified himself as the one fulfilling the prophecy from Isaiah, with a unique role of preparing the way for the Lord. His humble response emphasized the significance and privilege of his role, one that he would have missed had he been born earlier. As a forerunner, John directed people toward the coming Messiah, Jesus, playing a vital part in the unfolding narrative of salvation.

Indeed, there are many times when we witness God responding immediately to prayer—through His healing touch, His attentive ear, His divine intervention, and His miraculous works. I myself have experienced moments where God's guidance and help came swiftly, right after I cried out to Him. Scripture, too, is filled with countless examples of instant miracles—clear reminders that our God is both present and powerful.

When God Seems Silent: Lazarus

Yet, there are instances when, after fervent prayer, God appears to 'delay in responding,' presenting an air of apparent indifference. This scenario is reminiscent of the narrative in John 11 (NIV) where Lazarus falls seriously ill. Desperate, his sisters sent someone to implore Jesus for help. Upon receiving news of Lazarus's condition, Jesus chose to remain in His current location for an additional two days! Rather than hastening to heal Lazarus, Jesus informed the messengers, "This sickness will not end in death. No, it is for God's glory so that God's Son may be glorified through it." (v4) Understanding why Jesus exhibited what seems to be an 'unresponsive' reaction is challenging, particularly considering the deep love Jesus had for Lazarus and his sisters (v3). If I was Jesus, I would unquestionably have rushed to heal my beloved immediately—why wait for two more days?

When Jesus eventually decided to go and save Lazarus, regrettably, Lazarus had already passed away. In fact, by the time Jesus reached their home, Lazarus had been dead for four days! Nevertheless, Jesus performed a miraculous act by resurrecting Lazarus. Reflecting on the conclusion of this story, one might concur that God resurrecting Lazarus is even more miraculous and glorious than merely healing him. This narrative underscores that God is not only a healer but also a God who holds the power to resurrect, revealing the depth of His divine capabilities.

When God Does Not Heal: Elisha

There are instances when God does not seem to answer our prayers at all, leaving us with the question: Why? While I don't have a definite answer, I firmly believe in God's sovereignty, divine will, and overarching plan. The Old Testament, particularly the second Book of Kings specifically chapters 2 through 13, unfolds the narrative of Elisha. Elisha, a prophet and disciple of Elijah, succeeded the renowned Elijah, playing a pivotal role in numerous miracles and significant events. When Elijah passed away, Elisha inherited a double portion of Elijah's spirit, performing twice as many miracles as his predecessor. Elijah accomplished fourteen miracles; whereas Elisha, with this extraordinary anointing, went on to perform twenty-eight. Despite this extraordinary anointing, Elisha, in a tragic turn of events, succumbed to a fatal illness. The irony lies in the fact that, despite possessing a double portion of gifts compared to Elijah and having healed many and even raised the dead, Elisha could not save himself. It's a paradox that raises questions about the mysteries of God's ways.

Although the Bible does not explicitly detail whether Elisha prayed for his own illness, given his reputation as a devout prophet who frequently communicated with God, it seems implausible that he did not seek divine intervention for his ailment. The lingering question remains: Why did God allow Elisha to fall ill and eventually die rather than healing him? Unfortunately, I don't possess a definitive answer, as I am not God. However, if we delve into the aftermath of Elisha's death, we encounter a truly miraculous event: a dead body, upon contact with Elisha's bones, was resurrected (2 Kings 13:21). Isn't this an even more astonishing demonstration of God's power?

I am convinced that, regardless of the challenges we face and even if God doesn't intervene directly or in the midst of the most challenging situations, He can use those experiences to bring blessings to others. Perhaps God allowed Elisha to fall ill, experience death, and be buried so that a dead body, upon touching Elisha's bones, could be resurrected. Had Elisha been taken up to heaven like Elijah, this miraculous revival might never have occurred; truly, the ways of the Lord are profound and mysterious!

When God Listens and Responds: Hezekiah

You may wonder why we should still pray to God, considering His sovereignty, undisclosed plans, and the fact that His responses to our prayers may not align with our expectations. Let's explore 2 Kings 20:1–7 (NLT) for insight: 1 About that time Hezekiah became deathly ill, and the prophet Isaiah son of Amoz went to visit him. He gave the king this message: "This is what the Lord says: Set your affairs in order, for you are going to die. You will not recover from this illness."

2 When Hezekiah heard this, he turned his face to the wall and prayed to the Lord,

3 "Remember, O Lord, how I have always been faithful to you and have served you single-mindedly, always doing what pleases you." Then he broke down and wept bitterly.

4 But before Isaiah had left the middle courtyard, this message came to him from the Lord:

> 5 "Go back to Hezekiah, the leader of my people. Tell him, 'This is what the Lord, the God of your ancestor David, says: I have heard your prayer and seen your tears. I will heal you, and three days from now you will get out of bed and go to the Temple of the Lord.
>
> 6 I will add fifteen years to your life, and I will rescue you and this city from the king of Assyria. I will defend this city for my own honor and for the sake of my servant David.'" 7 Then Isaiah said, "Make an ointment from figs." So Hezekiah's servants spread the ointment over the boil, and Hezekiah recovered!

Hezekiah's story becomes a testament to the transformative power of prayer. Hezekiah was destined to die, as it was God's will. God had instructed the prophet Isaiah to inform him that he would die and not live any longer. However, Hezekiah did not give up. Even though he heard the prophet telling him that God wanted him to set his house in order because he would die, he turned to the wall and prayed to God. Who would have thought that God would change His will because of Hezekiah's prayer? Not only did Hezekiah not die from his illness, but God also added fifteen more years to his life! If Hezekiah had simply accepted the prophet's words and resigned himself to fate, he would have missed out on the miracle of God.

Drawing parallels from this narrative, the apostle Paul in 1 Thessalonians 5:16–18 (NLT) encourages believers to "Always be joyful. Never stop praying. Be thankful in all circumstances, for this is God's will for you who belong to Christ Jesus." Similarly, in Philippians 4:6–7, (NLT) Paul urges us "Don't worry about anything; instead, pray about everything. Tell God what you need, and thank him for all he has done. Then you will experience God's peace, which exceeds anything we can understand. His peace will guard your hearts and minds as you live in Christ Jesus."

Therefore, irrespective of life's trials, even in the darkest moments where hope seems elusive, believers are urged to emulate Hezekiah's resilience. As long as breath persists, the call is to persevere in prayer, unwaveringly trusting in God's mercy and intervention, for in prayer, we find a channel through which God's transformative miracles can unfold.

Part III: The Glory of God's Timing

This chapter is more than the testimony of salvation—it is the unveiling of heaven's orchestration, echoing the divine rhythm of promises fulfilled not in haste, but in perfect time. It reminds us that God's delays are not His denials, and that behind every prolonged silence, a splendour is being prepared.

Through years of longing, prayer, and patient intercession, the salvation of my parents became the crescendo of God's faithfulness. Like Zechariah, I questioned. Like Lazarus's sisters, I wept. But like Hezekiah, I chose to pray still. And now, like John the Baptist, I see the way made straight—not just for a nation, but for two precious souls I love.

Every story recounted—Zechariah, Lazarus, Elisha, Hezekiah—has whispered this singular truth: God's ways are higher, His timing flawless, His purposes glorious. The miraculous salvation of my parents, long thought improbable, became the shining jewel of God's mercy, testifying that no heart is too hard, no wait too long, no prayer unheard.

Let this chapter stand as an altar of remembrance: God is never late, and when He moves, the heavens declare His splendour.

Chapter 49

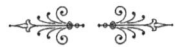

When A Teacher Found His Shepherd

After my parents accepted the Lord, my father no longer experienced those nightly visions. It was as though the divine messages had fulfilled their purpose, giving way to a new chapter—a chapter of growth, of prayer, and of walking with God. I gently began encouraging my parents to learn how to pray.

One evening, as we gathered around the dinner table, I invited my father to say grace. He looked at me, a little embarrassed, and said frankly, "I don't know how to pray." He passed the responsibility to my mother, who, without hesitation, offered a simple and heartfelt prayer.

The following morning, my mother shared something extraordinary. During the night, she had been awakened by an unusual sound. Thinking my father wanted to speak with her, she turned to find him still fast asleep. Yet from his lips came murmurs—soft, fluent utterances that resembled the clear, sweet chirping of a bird. It was a language she could not understand, melodic yet mysterious. She was deeply puzzled.

Could it have been sleep-talking? Or was it the Holy Spirit interceding through him in divine language, beyond human comprehension? As Romans 8:26 (ESV) says, "Likewise the Spirit helps us in our weakness. For we do not know what to pray for as we ought, but the Spirit himself intercedes for us with groanings too deep for words."

I remembered how my father had hesitated to pray just the evening before. But that night, God had moved. I believe the Holy Spirit came to him in his dreams, gently teaching him to pray, perhaps even using the heavenly language. Since that sacred moment, my father has never ceased to pray.

When my parents returned to Malaysia, my brother arranged for a local pastor to visit and follow up with them. The pastor invited them to church and encouraged them to join foundational Christian courses. Soon, my parents invited him into their home to help remove all the idols—a tangible step toward their newfound faith.

My father, ever methodical, wrote a prayer and taped it to the refrigerator door for my mother to follow if she wasn't sure what to say. Then, one day, while lifting a heavy iron plate to clear a drain, he injured his back. Ten painful days followed with no improvement; the pain worsened to the point where he feared it might be a stroke. Frustrated and unable to walk properly, he asked my mother which doctor he should consult. Busy in the kitchen, she didn't give a direct answer.

He hobbled to the living room and pondered which specialist to see. Then, unexpectedly, he thought of prayer. He prayed—not a short, desperate plea, but a long and earnest one. Eventually, he drifted off to sleep while still praying.

When he awoke, he resumed his chores. That evening at dinner, he realized he hadn't felt the back pain. The next morning, when he joined my mother for their daily walk with friends, he moved faster than usual—completely pain-free. It was a healing wrapped in humility and prayer. A lesson they had just learned in church had come alive in practice.

He now leads the family in prayer before meals, and the younger generations honour this practice. One day, when he was in the garden and the grandchildren were ready to eat, he told them to start without him. But the eldest grandchild went to the refrigerator, took the written prayer, and recited it faithfully before they began eating.

Whenever anyone in the family travels, he lifts up a prayer of protection and blessing. Faith has now become his rhythm.

Over forty-five years ago, my father relocated to Balakong, a quiet village of a couple of thousand residents to take up a teaching position at the local primary school. Throughout the decades, he became a respected figure, known and respected figure in the community. Today, as he walks those familiar streets and greets old friends, he shares more than memories—he shares the testimony of Christ.

One Sunday, the pastor invited him to share his journey of faith during the service. Standing at the pulpit, he addressed the congregation with quiet humility: "After teaching here for fifty years, and having moved here over forty-five years ago, I always knew about this church, but I had never stepped inside. You must be wondering why Mr. Chin is standing here today. Let me tell you why…"

In 2012, we celebrated my parents' golden wedding anniversary with a grand Thanksgiving banquet. Friends and family gathered from near and far, and my father stood proudly to share the testimony of how both he and my mother had come to accept Jesus.

Two years later, on Christmas Day 2014, I had the immense privilege of witnessing their water baptism. It was a profoundly emotional and holy moment—overflowing with joy, gratitude, and the quiet awe of answered prayer.

In that sacred moment, as I watched my parents step into the waters of baptism, I was overwhelmed. Years of prayer, hope, and quiet longing culminated in this beautiful act of surrender. It felt as though heaven had drawn near. I couldn't hold back the tears—not just of joy, but of deep reverence for God's faithfulness. Seeing my father and mother publicly declare their faith in Christ was one of the most meaningful moments of my life. It reminded me that no prayer is wasted, no heart is too hardened, and that God's timing, though often mysterious, is always perfect.

Acts 16:31 (NIV) declares, "Believe in the Lord Jesus, and you will be saved—you and your household." God's promises never fall to the ground; every word He utters is fulfilled. Since then, four of my siblings have accepted Jesus as their Saviour. Some remain on their own journey, but I trust in God's perfect timing. He continues to call them by name, for as 2 Peter 3:8–9 (NIV) reminds us, "With the Lord a day is like a thousand years, and a thousand years are like a day. The Lord is not slow in keeping his promise… He is patient… not wanting anyone to perish, but everyone to come to repentance."

And 1 Timothy 2:4 (NIV) affirms it clearly: God "wants all people to be saved and to come to a knowledge of the truth."

Indeed, the transformation in my father's life since he embraced the Lord is not only visible—it is radiant. His life has become a living psalm, a new song that rises like incense, fragrant and full of praise.

Chapter 50

The Divine Timeline

Time swiftly passes, and it has now been four decades since I first fell ill and underwent a bone marrow transplant. Forty years—a tapestry woven with trials, triumphs, transformation, and above all, grace. So many chapters have turned, too many to recount in full, yet my heart overflows with gratitude for the journey that has been.

Each time I pause and reflect on these passing years, my soul can only whisper, "Thank You"—to my loving Heavenly Father, the unseen hand who has never once let go. Through every shadow and every sunrise, He has walked with me, shaping every twist of the road according to His purpose. Not a moment wasted, not a sorrow unredeemed.

Kim and I have no achievements to boast of. The comfort and peace we enjoy today are not trophies of our own strength or wisdom. I do not wish to be called the luckiest man alive; I want to be known as the most blessed.

For this life is not built on chance—it rests upon a divine design. God does not merely wish for us to subscribe to a religion, but to enter into a relationship - reconciled, vibrant, purposeful and intimate. The nearer we draw to Him, the clearer we perceive His loving intentions.

I am grateful that when I was diagnosed with aplastic anaemia, though I challenged God to prove Himself by healing me instantly, He did not. He knew my heart too well. An immediate healing might have bred confusion: was it God, or the temple idols, or the Feng Shui master, or simply the medicine? Who would receive the glory? Instead, God chose a slower, wiser path that led me away from misplaced hopes and toward the living truth.

Even before I knew Him, God had already set His heart on me. His mercy chased me through the valley of illness, using the pain to draw me out of my comfort zone into a space where I could encounter Him. Like Abraham, who was called out of a land of idols to walk with the true God, so too was I called—out of uncertainty, into the arms of divine purpose.

God's delays are never denials. When He doesn't act at once, it is not from indifference. In my case, He did not send instant, miraculous healing—but through the bone marrow transplant, through restored fertility, and through the healing of my immune system, His fingerprints were everywhere. Every step, precisely timed.

I often think of the poem "Footprints in the Sand" by Mary Stevenson. In it, the dreamer sees two sets of footprints along the beach of life—until the hardest times, when only one set remains. "Why did You leave me when I needed You most?" the dreamer asks. And the Lord replies, "It was then that I carried you."

Such is the truth I've come to know. In the silence, He was there. In the loneliness, He was holding me. As Matthew 1:23 (NIV) reminds us, "They will call him Immanuel—which means, 'God with us.'" And Deuteronomy 31:8 (NIV) assures, "The Lord himself goes before you and will be with you; he will never leave you nor forsake you."

Looking back, I see now that the life Kim and I enjoy—our children, our family, our quiet moments of joy—are all reflections of God's glory. Jeremiah 29:11 (NIV) says, "For I know the plans I have for you," declares the Lord, "plans to prosper you and not to harm you, plans to give you hope and a future."

God's heart is never to harm, but to bless. Even what was meant for evil, He has turned for good. As Genesis 50:20 (NIV) says, "You intended to harm me, but God intended it for good to accomplish what is now being done, the saving of many lives."

These forty years have not merely been survival—they have been sacred. A testimony not of what I endured, but of the One who carried me through.

Chapter 51

The Divine Coincidence

How Every Seeming Accident Was Heaven's Design

My father's decision to transfer me to Yu Hua Primary School was not random. Being drawn to Kim during my second year at school was not accidental. It wasn't by mere chance that I, an ordinary young man, captured the heart of such an extraordinary girl. Nor was it coincidence that I was diagnosed with aplastic anaemia just after Kim genuinely revealed her feelings for me.

Doris, Kim's sister, immigrating to Australia at that precise time—wasn't that too perfectly timed to be chance? Peggy purchasing the apartment directly opposite the hospital just two months before our arrival—was that coincidence? The apartment's location, just steps away from the hospital, felt too intentional.

Contracting Hepatitis B through a transfusion in Malaysia—tragic, yes, but part of a mysterious design. Knowing the emergency number upon arriving in Australia wasn't luck. My father's immediate access to the hospital during a severe asthma attack was no random grace. Even the surreal chase by strange beings during his unconscious state, and the arrival of the remarkable physician who brought him back—surely, none of that happened by accident.

The complications I faced after surgery were no random misfortune. Ming and Fatt, whom we met while they lived undocumented in Australia—divine appointments. Lee's connection with colleagues who stepped in to help—an unseen hand. My repeated need to return to Australia for treatment was not just a medical necessity; it was a thread in the tapestry.

My insistence on applying for permanent residency, despite being flagged with a falsely recorded criminal offence in Malaysia, and enduring a three-year delay, none of it was arbitrary. Finding that small church tucked away on a side street in Manly, and all the seemingly ordinary events that followed in Sydney—each moment was part of a pattern, woven with purpose.

In her confusion after receiving the scholarship offer, Kim turned to the Bible for clarity. She found herself reading the passage where Jesus turned water into wine at the wedding in Cana. It was a quiet moment of reassurance—if Jesus could transform something so ordinary into something extraordinary, perhaps He was doing the same with her situation. That Scripture became a personal signpost. Accepting the scholarship and coming to Adelaide no longer felt like a random opportunity—it felt like a calling.

Every encounter, every hardship, every moment she endured in Adelaide became a thread in a greater tapestry. And just as she was about to graduate, I received news that my permanent residency had finally been approved. Could that be luck or timing? Or was it—as we've come to believe—God's quiet orchestration from the very beginning?

The message from the pastor on the radio, confirming that a child was on the way—heaven-sent. The moments when we opened the Bible and found immediate answers—divine whispers. My father's triple vision, just two days before Mr. Yu arrived to lead him to Christ—how could that be anything but supernatural? And the mysterious tongue of prayer, gifted to him in a dream—on the very night he confessed that he didn't know how to pray.

In short, nothing—absolutely nothing—in Kim's life or mine happened by accident. Because God has declared: *"For I know the plans I have for you," declares the Lord, "plans to prosper you and not to harm you, plans to give you hope and a future"* (Jeremiah 29:11, NIV).

It was all part of His divine script.

Even writing this testimony was no accident. And the fact that you are now reading these very words—this, too, is no coincidence. I began writing this book many years ago, but along the way, I grew discouraged. The right editor or publisher never came, and the dream faded.

There was a time I had given up. The dream of finishing this book lay dormant—like dry bones scattered across a forgotten valley. But I kept praying. Quietly. Weakly at times. That one day, the dry bones would come alive again.

And they did.

God, in His mercy, breathed life into what I thought was long dead. What you're holding in your hands is living proof of that breath—of prayers not wasted, of timing not missed, of stories still being written.

Then, just a month ago, during a Sunday service at church, I met a couple from Brisbane who were visiting their daughter, who was about to give birth. It was an unplanned, brief encounter. Yet in that short conversation, the husband shared that he had published a book about his own testimony. He encouraged me not to give up and introduced me to Art

House Publishing. That simple moment—so easily overlooked—reignited my conviction. The door reopened. The burden to complete this book returned, this time with a quiet urgency and clarity I hadn't felt in years.

Was that just chance? A passing conversation at church? Or was it—like so many other moments in this journey—another divine appointment, another piece of God's carefully woven plan?

And now, you are holding this book. Reading these words. That, too, may feel small—but I believe it's part of something much bigger. Perhaps God has been weaving a story in your life too, through encounters you didn't expect, delays you didn't understand, and moments that seemed insignificant—until now.

This is more than coincidence. This is the quiet evidence of a God who sees, who directs, and who writes every chapter with purpose.

If you find yourself sceptical, brushing aside all these divine timings as coincidences, even your finding this book may seem random. But I tell you: God is the Author of so-called coincidences. Every moment is His brushstroke on the canvas of your life—crafted to draw you closer, to open your heart, to reveal His love.

Behind what may appear as chance, God is calling. He seeks not just to bless us, but to make our lives a blessing to others. If you feel a stirring in your heart and long for the abundant life God has prepared for you, you can respond now with a simple prayer:

A Prayer of New Life

Almighty God, Creator of heaven and earth,
Thank You for Your immeasurable love and grace.
I confess that I am a sinner, falling short of Your glory.
Thank You for sending Your only Son, Jesus Christ,

To die on the cross for my sins,
And for raising Him on the third day.
Today, I receive Jesus as my Saviour.
I accept the forgiveness of my sins
And receive the gift of becoming Your beloved child.
Thank You, Father, for saving me.
I pray this in the victorious name of Jesus Christ, Amen.

If you have prayed this prayer—rejoice! You are now a child of God. Your heart may already be overflowing with peace, joy, and love that surpasses understanding.

Don't keep it to yourself. Share your decision with a Christian friend or pastor—they will celebrate with you. And so will I. And so will heaven. In fact, as Luke 15:10 (NIV) says, *"There is rejoicing in the presence of the angels of God over one sinner who repents."*

GOD BLESS YOU.

P.S. Thank you for taking the time to journey with me through these pages. If this testimony has encouraged your faith or stirred something in your heart, I would be humbled and grateful to hear from you. Please feel free to write to me at **thedivinecoincidence@gmail.com***.*

May God continue to lead and bless you in His perfect way.

About the Author

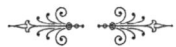

Tian Chin Born in Kajang, Malaysia, Tian Chin is the third of nine children and now calls Adelaide home. His story is one marked by miracles—each chapter filled with divine interventions that defied medical predictions and worldly expectations.

At 21, Tian was diagnosed with aplastic anaemia and given one year to live. After every treatment option in Malaysia was exhausted, he was flown to Sydney, where a bone marrow transplant from his younger sister gave him a second chance. Though the transplant saved his life, it ushered in decades of complications—hepatitis, graft-versus-host disease (GvHD), myasthenia gravis, and lung damage—alongside immigration challenges and the emotional weight of long-term recovery.

Yet at every turn, God provided: free housing during critical seasons, medical breakthroughs, immigration mercy—including the unexpected gift of permanent residency—and above all, spiritual transformation through a newfound faith in Jesus Christ.

In 1992, Tian married Kim, his high-school sweetheart and unwavering companion throughout years of illness and separation. Though doctors twice declared Tian infertile, they were blessed with three miracle children. And now, their testimony continues into a new generation with the arrival of their first grandchild—a living, breathing reminder that God's promises extend beyond what we can see.

Since 1990, Tian has been active in ministry among Mandarin-speaking communities in Sydney and Adelaide—leading connect groups, mentoring young families, translating sermons, and hosting international students with a gift for hospitality and heart-led care. He and Kim continue to co-lead a family group at Futures Church (formerly Paradise AOG, Paradise Community Church, and Influencers Church).

The Divine Coincidence is Tian's first memoir—a heartfelt reflection on faith, resilience, and the unmistakable fingerprints of God through every valley and breakthrough.

Epilogue: Forty Years of Grace

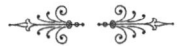

This year, 2025, marks the 40th anniversary of my bone marrow transplant, a milestone that whispers of mercy, endurance, and miracles too vast to count. Time, like a swift river, has carried me through seasons of hardship and healing, sorrow and splendour.

In Scripture, the number forty is never arbitrary. It represents testing, transformation, and divine preparation. Noah faced 40 days of rain. Moses spent 40 years in the wilderness. The Israelites wandered for 40 years before entering the Promised Land. Jesus fasted 40 days before beginning His public ministry. And now, I find myself standing on the other side of forty—forty years since my own trial began. This is not just an anniversary. It is a sacred marker of God's faithfulness.

We remain rooted in Adelaide, faithfully attending what is now known as Futures Church, the same community we've called home since settling here. We continue to serve as connect group leaders—still walking with others, still walking with God.

Our journey has not only continued - it has blossomed.

Two of our beloved children have entered into the sacred bond of marriage:

Annabelle, now a compassionate sonographer, is married to Nick, an accountant.

Joshua, our pilot soaring through the skies, is wed to Clara, a marketing coordinator. They are now proud parents to their beautiful daughter, Charlotte Grace—a precious new chapter and blessing for our family.

And Faith, our youngest, an Oral Health Therapist, walks joyfully in a blossoming relationship.

All three of our children not only know the Lord, they serve Him—rooted in the same church that nurtured our own faith. This is no small miracle. It is a testimony, not to our parenting, but to the faithfulness of a covenant-keeping God.

As for me and my household, we will serve the Lord (Joshua 24:15, NIV).

While Kim is still enjoying her work as an accountant, I have now entered into retirement—gratefully, peacefully. We are deeply grateful to witness God's generational blessing unfolding through our first grandchild, Charlotte Grace.

Physically, my journey carries remnants of the battle. My immune system is now considered stable, though a trace of graft-versus-host disease remains in my mouth. Lung scarring has left me with around 50 percent function—a reality that once brought deep concern during the pandemic. Yet by God's mercy, even after contracting COVID-19 twice, I experienced only mild symptoms. I don't take that lightly. Every breath I draw is a quiet miracle, a reminder that healing isn't always about full restoration, but about being upheld daily by His strength. I am still here—not because I am strong, but because He is.

My heart overflows with gratitude—not for a life devoid of hardship, but for a life so visibly marked by God's hand. From the quiet hospital rooms where life and death danced, to joyful celebrations of weddings and baptisms, from moments of doubt to glorious awakenings, I have seen the goodness of the Lord in the land of the living.

To share this story—with you—is itself a gift beyond measure.

EPILOGUE: FORTY YEARS OF GRACE

Not chance.
Not coincidence.
But *The Divine Coincidence*—love arranged in heaven's perfect order.
To God be the glory - now and forever.

Let every divine coincidence in this book remind readers that God never forgets, delays without purpose, or wastes any part of our story. This book, this testimony, was never just about recovery. It's about redemption. May your own journey, too, be marked by divine coincidences—each one drawing you closer to the Author of your story.

www.ingramcontent.com/pod-product-compliance
Lightning Source LLC
Chambersburg PA
CBHW032111090426
42743CB00007B/311